PSYCHOLOGY WORLDS ISSUE 34

CONNOR WHITELEY

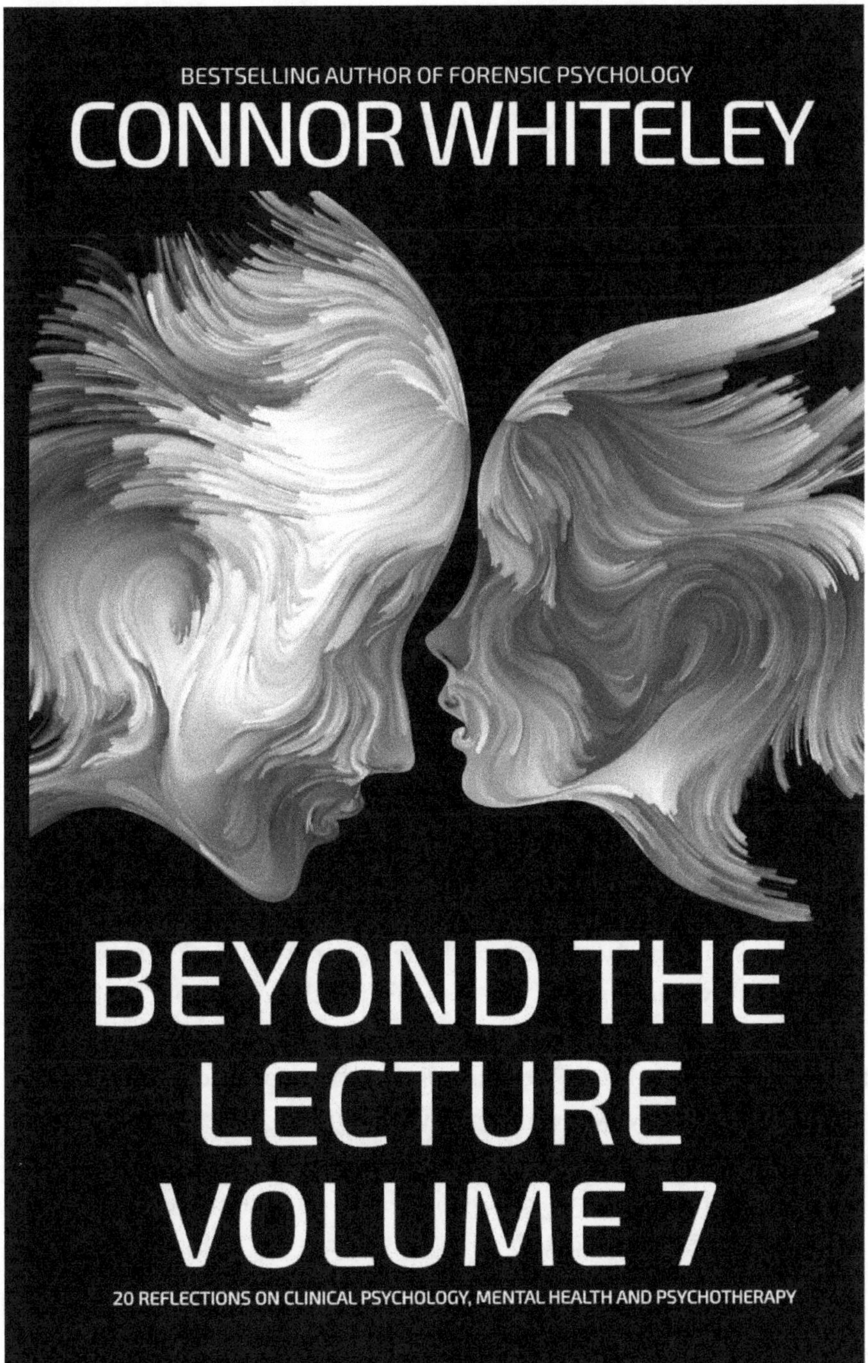

BESTSELLING AUTHOR OF FORENSIC PSYCHOLOGY
CONNOR WHITELEY
BEYOND THE LECTURE VOLUME 7
20 REFLECTIONS ON CLINICAL PSYCHOLOGY, MENTAL HEALTH AND PSYCHOTHERAPY

INTRODUCTION

October is always an exciting time in the psychology calendar. If you're a psychology student then it's the "real" start of another university year filled with new learning, making new friends and making new great memories together. I miss those times and some of the best years of my life were at university.

If you're an aspiring or qualified psychologist, then October might be another day at the office to you. Yet it is also the start of the final quarter of the year. It is a chance for you to start wrapping up 2025, start planning what you want to achieve in 2026 and most importantly, how do you want to progress your psychology career.

Personally, I'm rather excited for October 2025 because I get to start my first job after finishing up my Masters in Clinical Psychology. I'll be starting as a teaching assistant in a special educational needs school. I'm excited to start because it should be fun, filled with learning experiences and it will help me get the clinical experience I need to progress my psychology journey.

October has a lot to look forward to.

Speaking of learning and progressing your psychology career, this issue of the Psychology World Magazine is packed full of great content, psychology articles and books to help deepen your understanding of this amazing field.

Kicking off the issue is *What is Radicalisation and What Are The Signs in Children.* Originally, I researched, wrote up and produced this article because I knew this was going to be one of the interview questions for a job in education that I went for. There's a lot more to radicalisation in children than the media and common sense would have you believe, so if you want to work in education, with children or you want to know more about this forensic psychology topic. This article will be brilliant for you. It's engaging, in-depth and fascinating.

Secondly, in *What is Media Psychology*, you get to learn about another, rather new area of psychology that you can work in. In psychology, we tend to focus on clinical, educational and other applied aspects of psychology but media psychology isn't really spoken about. That's what I aim to change in this insightful, thoughtful and riveting psychology article that might make you want to change career paths.

It certainly made me question my career for a few days.

Thirdly, *What To Do When Depression Makes it Impossible To Get Out of Bed* is a more practical podcast episode filled with tips and techniques to help people with depression to get out of bed. You'll learn why depression makes it impossible in the first place, how people with depression can overcome this difficulty and what the implications are for aspiring and qualified psychologists. If you want to work with people with depression, then this fun article is a must-read.

Penultimately, we take a brief break from clinical psychology and turn our attention towards social and developmental psychology in *Are Infants Moral*. This article was so surprising, so much fun and it definitely makes you question a lot of your assumptions about children, morality and more. You won't be disappointed by this article.

Our final article in this issue is *What is Social Prescribing*. This was another article inspired by a job interview that I went for after graduating from my MSc. It isn't a strictly psychology-focused role but it draws on a lot of mental health concepts, it requires applying psychology in the real world and most importantly, it's about improving lives.

The entire point of clinical psychology after all.

Moving on to the book section of the issue, *The Forensic Psychology of Terrorism and Hostage-Taking* returns to these pages proudly. I loved writing, researching and creating this book because it helps you to understand the issues with terrorism research, what actually makes someone into a terrorist instead of what the media and governments would like you to believe and so much more. This was fascinating, insightful and I learnt tons from this book.

And the really fun thing about this book is that it allows you to apply this research to the news, everyday life and it makes you question why governments and military commanders take certain actions. Since it will only increase terrorist recruitment instead of annihilating it like militaries and governments claim they will.

Finally, for the first time, *Your Unshakable Self* makes its impressive debut in these pages. There is so much I could say about this international bestselling book, but I don't want to spoil it. Therefore, all I will say is that if you want to understand who you are, your sense of self and if you want to feel whole, especially after experiencing trauma, then this will be a life-changing book for you.

I know the content of this book changed my life for the better, my mental health has improved dramatically and it was a lot of fun to research, learn about and write.

You will learn so much in this issue.

Therefore, now that we know about all the great articles and books in this issue, let's turn over the page and start exploring some psychology worlds.

WHAT IS RADICALISATION AND WHAT ARE THE SIGNS OF RADICALISATION IN CHILDREN?

Next week at the time of writing, I have a job interview and one of the questions relates to what are the signs of radicalisation in children. The interview is for a learning support assistant role at a local school and the UK Government makes it a legal requirement for workers in education to Prevent radicalisation in children, so this is a part of that duty of care. In addition, whilst we've previously learnt about terrorism and other related criminal psychology topics on the podcast, we haven't learnt about radicalisation too much before now. Therefore, in this forensic psychology podcast episode, you'll learn what is radicalisation, what are the signs of radicalisation in children and why is radicalisation in children important to learn about. If you enjoy learning about terrorism, radicalisation and criminal psychology then this will be a great episode for you.

What Is Radicalisation?

Previously I think it is fair to say, in our ignorance as a society, we only needed to be concerned about children being radicalised by Islamic extremists, because this was the narrative that was pushed onto us. Yet now we understand that radicalisation can happen towards any ideology including Incels, far-right, misogyny, white supremacy and on and on and on. There are lot of different destructive, far-right ideologies that young people can be radicalised by and as educators and aspiring and qualified psychologists, we need to be aware of radicalisation and the signs.

Once we recognise the signs of radicalisation then we need to support our young people so they do not adopt these toxic, destructive ideologies and ultimately do not take up action against these innocent minority groups based on the lies of others. For example, when Incels demand and shoot up women because of incels' toxic and ill-informed beliefs.

As a result, radicalisation is the process where anyone, including adults, starts to support and/ or get involved in extremist ideologies. These ideologies are normally political or religious but they can be made up of other beliefs too. For instance, I don't think incel or white supremacy beliefs are based on religion and they are political to a point, but not really. I think incel beliefs in particular are based on social beliefs.

Anyway, radicalisation can be devastating to children, their families as well as their communities. People might be tempted to believe that radicalisation is only about beliefs, so cognitive processes, but we know that our cognitive processes can lead to action and behaviours in the right situation. Therefore, radicalisation can lead to physical and violent behaviours, like shooting up a group of black people, and this is why it is critical to help protect children and young people against radicalisation.

In addition, children tend to be the focus of anti-radicalisation work because young people are more likely to be radicalised compared to other age groups. Since their worldview is still developing and their worldview can influence their relationships, decisions and future prospects. For instance, if a young person gets involved in white supremacy during their teenage years, they become racist and physically violent towards black people and they beat a black person within an inch of their life. Then they will hopefully be arrested, charged and sent to prison for assault. Equally, I hope they will be deradicalized too. Yet because of their violent behaviour, they've lost years of their life, they have a criminal record and this will impact their employability and the rest of their life.

This is all because of radicalisation.

What Is The Process of Radicalisation?

Despite the path towards radicalisation being slightly different for everyone, there are a lot of patterns that set a child or young person down the similar, gradual path towards becoming radicalised. Firstly, a child is exposed to extremist ideas through online forums, friends, community groups, family members or social media. As well as sometimes, extremists actively target vulnerable young people to recruit them to the cause and this isn't exclusive to Islamic extremist groups like the mainstream narrative would have us believe.

Also, as I talk about in my book, *Applied*

Psychology, there are a lot of different factors that can lead someone towards radicalisation. These include, low self-esteem, feelings of injustice, social isolation as well as need to belong.

Generally, the four key stages of radicalisation are Exposure so a child is exposed to the extremist beliefs or materials for the first time. Engagement is when the young person starts to show an interest in these beliefs and starts to explore these ideas further. Thirdly, you have adoption where the young person adopts these extremist beliefs as their own. Finally, you have action where the young person takes steps towards supporting and/ or openly participating in extremist activity. This includes donating money or sharing videos and other content online or joining the extremist organisation.

To use an example of the white supremacy, a young person might see a meme online that they find funny. Then the young person might explore these white supremacy memes, online videos and racist comments in more depth and want to understand white supremacy. Afterwards, the young person starts to agree with white supremacy and starts to take on the racist beliefs as their own. Finally, the young person might start sharing racist videos online, talking to their friends about racist views and why non-whites are plaguing society and they might vote for racist candidates or donate money towards racist organisations. As well as they might campaign against non-whites living in their area.

<u>What Are The Signs of Radicalisation?</u>

This is the section I'm really interested in because of my job interview next week and I strongly believe at first when we think about the signs of radicalisation, there are the "clear" ones. You might associate being alone, vulnerable and physically aggressive as signs of radicalisation and that's true. Yet there are so many more signs of radicalisation too.

Moreover, it's useful to note that whilst some of the signs of radicalisation might be crystal clear, like glorifying extremist figures, showing beliefs in conspiracy theories and using extremist language. A lot of the other signs of radicalisation are a lot more subtle and they develop over time as well as some of these signs are perfectly normal when they occur alone.

Nonetheless, it is when these signs occur together and there are changes in behaviour, that is when there is cause for concern that the child might be at risk of radicalisation.

A first sign of radicalisation is that a child or young person loses interest in their schoolwork and normal hobbies. That on its own doesn't sound too bad because most children don't want to be at school, focus on their schoolwork and one of the symptoms of depression is that you lose pleasure and interest in things you used to enjoy. Yet when we consider other signs this is a lot more alarming.

Another sign of radicalisation is that child or young person becomes withdrawn and/ or they spend more time than normal alone. Again, it doesn't sound too alarming and there are some children who are naturally more lonely than others. When I was a kid, I could have been called lonely because I didn't have many friends, I didn't hang out with anyone after school amongst other reasons, except my friends in the Sea Scouts.

Yet what makes losing interest in schoolwork and normal hobbies and withdrawn signs of radicalisation is that they make young people long for connection and friends. Sadly, extremist ideologies can seem very tempting and the manipulators and recruiters behind these ideologies are very skilled at convincing young people that this is where they belong.

A third sign of radicalisation is when young people use language that mirrors extremist rhetoric or their language sounds scripted. This isn't one that I've heard before but I completely agree thinking back to online clips I've seen then blocked. It's why I don't go on Twitter much these days. It's just a far-right breeding ground as far as I'm concerned. Believers in extremist ideologies always sound the same because they use the scripted language that they've learnt online from other people to support their extremist views and defend their beliefs against other people trying to challenge them.

A fourth sign is that a young person or child might show increase frustration, obsessive behaviour and anger. Again, these extremist ideologies are very effective at inciting, tapping into hate and cultivating anger within people. You only need to look at the UK politics this week to see how the major political parties are using immigration and refugees as the scapegoat for Westminster's issues. Instead immigrants aren't the issue because personally what annoys me as a rape survivor is that there are thousands of rapes every year in the UK. Yet the few times an immigrant commits sexual violence everyone goes mad, but my rapist was a white man and no one cared.

Anyway, this isn't a political show and I've likely already annoyed enough people so let's continue.

Additionally, other signs of radicalisation include sharing hateful views, memes, content and symbols on social media, spending more time online and becoming increasingly disrespectful and intolerant of other people and their different viewpoints. Personally, even though I am steadfast in my views, I still like to hear, listen and try to understand other people and were they're coming from. I will likely never agree with these viewpoints but I am interested in listening and just because people hold different beliefs to me, it doesn't automatically make them bad people. Radicalised people do not believe in that and they will not tolerate people with differing views.

Penultimately, another sign of radicalisation is that a young person will show more of a focus on one subject, like a given political conflict or immigration. If we look at the far-right, they are always focusing on immigration because they do not care about the evidence that shows higher immigration levels do NOT lead to increases in sexual violence, and immigrants do not drain the benefit system and so on.

A final sign of radicalisation is that a young person changes their friendship groups suddenly. On its own, this might not seem like a major concern because it's normal for children and young people to change social groups and identities like clothing, but when you combine this sign with the other signs of radicalisation. Then this can get a lot more concerning. Especially, if there is already a social group at school that is known for their racist viewpoints and new young people are joining that friendship group.

Conclusion

Ultimately, talking about radicalisation and extremism is never a fun topic and it is always heart-wrenching to know that there are people out there and extremist ideologies that want to harm our young people. There are monsters out there that want to take advantage of the loneliness, mental health difficulties and need to belong that drives all of us, including our children. This is why it's important that we talk about radicalisation and most importantly how to recognise the signs of radicalisation, so we can support our young people and hopefully deradicalise them.

In addition, to prevent radicalisation, some general tips and techniques include teaching children how to critically think about the information they hear and see online, helping children and young people understand how to verify online content through media literacy skills, and creating a safe space for a healthy discussion and debate round controversial topics.

Going back to my last point, I know it is tempting for teachers, schools and parents to simply avoid talking about controversial topics. Yet in my experience, children and young people will have these conversations regardless so it is better to have them in a school where they can be controlled, tailored and fact-checked than online when extremist ideologies can come in and taint and twist the entire conversation towards their extremist agenda.

In addition, you can prevent radicalisation by providing a confidential support system where students can express concerns in private, you can help children to build resilience so young people can challenge extremist narratives and help parents become more aware of online risks as well as the signs of radicalisation too.

You also need to report a child being at risk of radicalisation to the safeguarding officer at your organisation and education setting too.

Finally, even though radicalisation from Islamic extremists hasn't been on the news so much in recent years. This really doesn't mean radicalisation is over and our children and our young people aren't at risk anymore. Instead children and young people are now at risk of white supremacy, the far right, the anti-immigration, misogynists, incels and manosphere and so many other extremist threats that radicalisation is still very present, very real and it can be very devastating to our children.

This is why we need to learn the signs, support children at risk of radicalisation and always focus on preventing radicalisation as much as possible.

Criminal Psychology Reference and Further Reading

Cherney, A., Belton, E., Norham, S. A. B., & Milts, J. (2022). Understanding youth radicalisation: an analysis of Australian data. *Behavioral Sciences of Terrorism and Political Aggression, 14*(2), 97-119.

Daher, L. M., Gamuzza, A., Mavica, G., Nicolosi, D., & Bontà, C. (2025). Youth Agency and Radicalisation: Unpacking the Voices, Hopes and Complexities of Embodied Subjectivity. *Social Roots of Violent Extremism: Pathways and Trends in Europe*, 57.

Espenschied, M. J. (2024). *The radicalisation of youth: the contagion of ideologically motivated violent extremism throughout COVID-19* (Doctoral dissertation, Macquarie University).

Heinze, A. S. (2025). Drivers of radicalisation? The development and role of the far-right youth organisation 'Young Alternative'in Germany. *International Political Science Review*, *46*(1), 108-124.

https://www.highspeedtraining.co.uk/hub/what-does-radicalisation-mean

Parker, D., Lindekilde, L., & Gøtzsche-Astrup, O. (2021). Recognising and responding to radicalisation at the 'frontline': Assessing the capability of school teachers to recognise and respond to radicalisation. *British Educational Research Journal*, *47*(3), 634-653.

Sjøen, M. M., & Mattsson, C. (2020). Preventing radicalisation in Norwegian schools: How teachers respond to counter-radicalisation efforts. *Critical studies on terrorism*, *13*(2), 218-236.

Taylor, L., & Soni, A. (2017). Preventing radicalisation: a systematic review of literature considering the lived experiences of the UK's Prevent strategy in educational settings. *Pastoral Care in Education*, *35*(4), 241-252.

Whiteley, C. (2024) Forensic Psychology of Terrorism And Hostage-Taking. *CGD Publishing. England.*

WHAT IS MEDIA PSYCHOLOGY?

I first became aware of media psychology in 2024 when I kept seeing media psychology training courses being advertised in The Psychologist magazine by the British Psychology Society. I had never heard of media psychology before but I checked out the courses and £100 wasn't a bad price. In the future, I might take one of the courses so I can deepen my understanding of what is media psychology, what do media psychologists do and the various roles that media psychologists play on production sets. However, until that time, in this cyberpsychology podcast episode, you'll explore what is media psychology, what topics do media psychologists study and more. If you're interested in the intersection between applied psychology, careers in psychology and technology then this will be a brilliant podcast episode for you.

What is Media Psychology?

As you might be aware because media psychology isn't well-known, it is certainly a newer branch of psychology compared to others, like cognitive psychology and behaviourism. Media psychology focuses on investigating how people are impacted by technology as well as the media.

In addition, media psychology is important because we are constantly surrounded by media. Even now surround me as I write this episode, I have my wireless earphones in my ears blasting some Demonslayer music as I struggle to keep some my anxiety out of my head about telling my partner tomorrow that I am a rape survivor. I have my laptop to one side with my monitor with this Word Document and my research on another screen. As well as I have my phone next to my mouse, so even though I am working right now. I am still surrounded by technology. And even beforehand I picked today's topic, I was reading some short stories on my tablet.

We are surrounded by technology.

As a result, it's important that psychology understands the impact that technology has on. Also, media psychology is very interdisciplinary because the constant changes in how people interact with technology which makes this particular area of study difficult to define. In my opinion, this is even more relevant because we are seeing how people change their search and digital consumption patterns with the rise of artificial intelligence. As well as how the artificial intelligence is revolutionising and changing companies and the workplace.

Building upon this, media psychology is heavily influenced by obviously psychology, but academia focusing on communication too. Like, sociology, anthropology, fan studies and media studies. Because of this, a lot of media psychology researchers don't consider psychology to be their main area of research because they believe their main research area is media's influence on individuals rather than a subtopic within a larger subject of expertise.

Interestingly, last month I went to a postgraduate talk on Taylor Swift and feminism, and looking back, I suppose this is largely about how individuals interact with her music, her messages and her as a fan culture. The lecturer giving the talk was a Doctor of English Literature and she gave a brilliant talk. Yet it is interesting to think about how English Literature in this situation could fall under the umbrella of psychology because she was studying texts and lyrics to see why Taylor Swift has the impact she does on individuals.

Ultimately, according to The Oxford Handbook of Media Psychology, the discipline is defined as "Media psychology is the scientific study of human behaviour, thoughts and feelings experienced in the context of media use and creation,"

What Does Media Psychology Study?

We already know media psychology focuses on investigating the interaction between people and technology, but here are some specific topics that media psychologists can study. Online learning is a topic of interest because it helps media psychologists to understand the impact of online teaching, for example, and how in-person lessons can be enhanced by technology or adapted for online teaching. As well as how media messages can be constructed to encourage someone to give to a charity or do another prosocial behaviour.

Media influence is another topic that media psychologists get excited by. They could investigate the impact of how exposure to media depictions of violence might or might not increase aggression, how depictions of gender roles impact sexist attitudes or perpetuates harmful gender stereotypes and so on.

In addition, media psychologists investigate audience involvement. Such as, why do we cry or laugh at certain moments in a TV programme or film? How do stories impact our sense of self, our identity and our social norms? As well as why do popular culture fans come together to form supportive or sometimes toxic communities?

Personally, given how I live with three people who flat out love Minecraft and I constantly hear about different things they're doing in Minecraft, and streamers are popular in legal trouble and so on. I would be interested in knowing how Minecraft developed such a cult following.

One final topic of interest is the impact of social media. Media psychologists investigate how social media platforms could create more comprehensive view of the world instead of an echo-chamber that amplifies hate and toxic body image ideals. As well as researchers could investigate how different types of social media use can impact mental health conditions, like depression and anxiety. If you want to learn more about social media use definitely check out my book Social Media Psychology.

How Did Media Psychology Develop?

Interestingly, media psychology isn't as new as everyone thinks it is because Hugo Munsterberg was the first person to look empirically at how an audience responded to film in his 1916 book *The Photoplay: A Psychological Study*. Then it came into the mainstream a little more in the 1950s when psychologists started to look more into how media impacted children.

Nonetheless, media psychology itself wasn't brought into the mainstream until 1986 when the American Psychological Association established the Media Psychology division as the organisation's 46th division. When it first started, it was focused on psychologists who appeared in the media as expert witnesses and sources of information. This is still somewhat the function of the division today but it has changed its name to the Society for Media Psychology and Technology in the United States. Its current modern focus is researching the effects and influence of media.

Finally, whilst in recent years the field has expanded to include various journals focusing on media psychology and there is an increase in universities dedicated modules, courses and research into media psychology. In 2003, the only APA-accredited (and this was still true as of 2023) media psychology PhD programme was at the Fielding Graduate University.

What Are Some Careers in Media Psychology?

It is certainly true that other areas of psychology have better defined career routes but media psychology has a few options for people. Media psychologists becoming an academic researcher is very normal and it is the standard career route. One reason why media psychology doesn't have a lot of defined career routes at the moment is because it is still so new and the discipline is still defining its scope as well as purview.

However, the context I always see media psychologists being employed is on TV and Film production crews. This is important because in an ever-expanding world of technology, this represents a chance for a lot of opportunities to apply media psychology in a wide range of industries from TV to film to education as well as politics. Everyone wants to know about how technology impacts us so they can create better health and safety rules, laws and regulations that better protect people.

I'll be surprised if people aren't familiar with Love Island (and no before you ask, I do not watch it but it is impossible not to be aware of it in the UK). Yet I know reality TV programmes like Love Island are starting to employ media psychologists to better help them protect the mental health of their contestants.

Moreover, media psychologists are important for teaching children lessons in media as well as cyberliteracy from a young age. In these situations, media psychologists are very useful because they can be the experts in designing and implementing these programmes.

Conclusion: What Is The Future Of Media Psychology?

In this cyberpsychology podcast episode, we've learnt that media psychology investigates how people are impacted by technology as well as the media. Also, whilst early media psychology research focused on the negative impacts of media, it is important to recognise that modern media psychology recognises that media and technology isn't all good nor all bad. What matters is how we use technology and with the constantly changing nature of technology and media, all of us as individuals and as a society, we must learn how to maximise the positives of technology whilst minimising the negatives.

Thankfully, this is where media psychologists come in because they play a critical role in helping our understanding of how to navigate these developments. Which in the current world because artificial intelligence, let alone other forms of technology and media, changes and advances weekly. The job of media psychologists is more important than ever.

Therefore, when it comes to the future of media psychology, I think the discipline will only grow in popularity and importance as we look to examine the positives and negatives of new forms of media and technology and how they impact individuals. Then as we race to catch up with technology in terms of laws, regulations and Acts of Parliament, we need to use media psychologists to advise us, production companies and governments about how best to protect people.

Because for me, that is the entire point of psychology, psychology is a force for good and I strongly believe media psychology is flat out critical for the future.

So if you're interested in understanding how the media impacts people then maybe check out courses and careers in media psychology.

You never know what weird, wonderful and fascinating places it might lead you.

Cyberpsychology Psychology References and Further Reading

Brown Rutledge P. Arguing for Media Psychology as a Distinct Field. In: Dill KE, ed. The Oxford Handbook Of Media Psychology. 1st ed. Oxford University Press; 2012.

Cummings, J. J., & Bailenson, J. N. (2016). How immersive is enough? A meta-analysis of the effect of immersive technology on user presence. Media psychology, 19(2), 272-309.

Dill, KE. Introduction. In: Dill KE, ed. The Oxford Handbook Of Media Psychology. 1st ed. Oxford University Press; 2012.

Fischoff S. Media Psychology: A Personal

Essay in Definition and Purview. J Media Psychol. 2005;10(1):1-21.

Kleemans, M., Daalmans, S., Carbaat, I., & Anschütz, D. (2018). Picture perfect: The direct effect of manipulated Instagram photos on body image in adolescent girls. Media Psychology, 21(1), 93-110.

Skowronski, M., Busching, R., & Krahé, B. (2021). Links between exposure to sexualized Instagram images and body image concerns in girls and boys. Journal of Media Psychology.

Stever GS. Media and Media Psychology. In: Stever GS, Giles DC, Cohen JD, Myers ME. Understanding Media Psychology. 1st ed. New York: Routledge; 2021:1-13.

Sundar, S. S., Jia, H., Waddell, T. F., & Huang, Y. (2015). Toward a theory of interactive media effects (TIME) four models for explaining how interface features affect user psychology. The handbook of the psychology of communication technology, 47-86.

Tuma RM. Media Psychology and Its History. In: Dill KE, ed. The Oxford Handbook Of Media Psychology. 1st ed. Oxford University Press; 2012.

Valkenburg, P. M., Peter, J., & Walther, J. B. (2016). Media effects: Theory and research. Annual review of psychology, 67(1), 315-338.

Wallace, P. (2015). The psychology of the Internet. Cambridge University Press.

AVAILABLE AT ALL MAJOR BOOKSELLERS!

WHAT TO DO WHEN DEPRESSION MAKES IT IMPOSSIBLE TO GET OUT OF BED

With depression being one of the most common mental health conditions in the world, a lot of a clinical psychologist's workload will be supporting people with depression. A common depression symptom is what's known as "Leaden Paralysis" and one of the effects of the symptoms is that everyday tasks take a million times more energy to complete. This can make the "simple" task of getting out of bed feel impossible for people with depression. Therefore, in this clinical psychology podcast episode, you'll learn what is leaden paralysis, why leaden paralysis impacts people's mental health and what to do when depression makes it impossible to get out of bed. If you enjoy learning about mental health, Major Depressive Disorder and psychotherapy then this will be a great episode for you.

Note: nothing in this book is ever any sort of official medical, mental health, relationship or any other form of advice.

What is The Weight of Depression?

If you've ever experienced depression then you might be aware that there are some days where your depression will weigh you down so much that it feels like your body is made of lead and concrete. This makes the very notion of doing anything, much less leave your bed feel flat out impossible. As well as the sheer weight of depression might make you cancel plans, spend more time at home and/ or you might miss or be late for work.

This weight of depression and a struggle to get out of bed can take a massive toll on your work, relationships and your quality of life.

Personally, during August until October 2024 when I had quite severe depression, it always took me about two hours to get out of bed in the morning. Getting out of bed just felt hard because I had fun things to do, I could see my friends and everything but it wasn't good enough motivation to actually want to get out of bed. I just wanted the day to be over so I could sleep and I didn't have to deal with all the trauma responses that I was having every single hour of every single day.

What Is Leaden Paralysis?

As a result, there is a symptom of depression called "leaden paralysis" that causes people with depression to experience a severe drop in energy and as Qi et al. (2020) highlights this makes everyday tasks a million times harder for the individual. This is important to bear in mind because a lot of people who have never experienced depression or severe depression before might argue that people should just get up. Yet it isn't that easy. And this is one of the reasons why depression is a leading cause of disability round the world (Friedrich, 2017).

One of the clearest examples for me of leaden paralysis was on the very first day of my severe depression when it took me 5 hours just to have a shower. After struggling to get up for two or three hours, I managed to eventually make breakfast and at midday I decided to try to have a shower. Yet everything felt so heavy, I was so drained, I had no energy and my body might as well have had 20kg kettlebells tied to it.

It took so long to go through the living room, up the stairs, grab my towel and clothes, go across the landing, go into the bathroom, undressed, etc, etc.

Every one of those steps felt so impossible and each one took so long.

That is what leaden paralysis is like and that's why supporting people with depression is so important. You can probably imagine but having leaden paralysis doesn't make you feel great and it can make you feel even worse about yourself as your quality of life starts to crumble, so this is why mental health support is critical.

What To Do When Depression Makes It Impossible To Get Out Of Bed?

Here are three strategies to help people with depression overcome leaden paralysis and get out of bed in the mornings.

Firstly, you can break the day down into "hoops". This strategy involves breaking down your day into sections then you visualise these tasks as hoops. For example, getting up or brushing your teeth can be seen as two hoops that need to be conquered. After completing each task, you could imagine yourself jumping through each hoop and this can be an encouraging visual so you get a sense of achievement, and it helps to make the day less overwhelming. As well as on the really difficult days, seeing tasks as hoops can help you determine what tasks or hoops can be done on other days.

Secondly, you need to try to be kind to yourself because one of the ways how depression impacts us is makes us criticise ourselves more often. Therefore, to define your depression and how it criticizes you every chance it gets, you might want to practise self-kindness by using compassionate words when you realise your self-dialogue is getting more negative and harsher.

For example, today is actually a good example for me because my mental health definitely dipped today, and I was tired, overwhelmed and I was anxious about seeing my partner tomorrow because of trauma responses. My partner has done nothing wrong by the way. This meant I didn't get up for over an hour this morning and when I had a nap in the late afternoon in an effort to make myself feel better, I napped for 40 minutes but I didn't get out of bed for another two hours.

At first I was judging myself harshly because that was such a waste of time, I had so much to do and on and on and on. But I realised that it's okay I couldn't get out of bed earlier because this is what happens when my mental health dips. I need to listen to myself, figure out what's causing my mental health to dip and just keep going. Things will get better later on or tomorrow and as long as I focus on just going forward then that's okay. As well as I am hardly alone because this happens to everyone at different times in their life, even more so when you have depression and other mental health difficulties.

This is what works for me, you might need other self-compassionate and self-kindness thoughts.

The key is to not feed into your depression by criticising and hating yourself because you can't get out of bed. This will only make it feel even harder to do everyday tasks.

Finally, reach out for mental health support, because if you're experiencing depression that is so severe you find it really difficult to get out of bed. It is important that you seek mental health support as soon as possible because if you don't get support then your symptoms might get worse and your risk of suicide and self-harm increase. I really don't want that for you. As well as your depression might make you want to be alone and isolate yourself, but when you're struggling, it is a really good idea to be surrounded by other people. These people can include friends and family, but make sure you reach out to mental health professionals like a therapist or a mental health helpline too. Since if you isolate yourself then you might quickly find yourself in an echo chamber surrounded by your negative thoughts and inactivity and this will only maintain your depression.

And make you feel worse and worse until you don't see another way out.

Whenever I go through depression and mental health difficulties, reaching out to mental health support is always the best thing I could have done. It is always nerve-racking, I try to put it off as long as possible and I try to deal with things on my own at first. Yet ultimately seeing a counsellor, therapist or another form of mental health support is always best and I grow and develop so much and I flat out love the process too.

Conclusion

Whether you're a aspiring or qualified psychologist or person with depression, we've learnt a lot during today's psychology podcast episode. For psychologists, a lot of our future work will be with people with depression and we will encounter leaden paralysis the majority of the time because it is a common symptom. I know as someone who has experienced the inability to get out of bed frequently in the past, this is very distressing, it makes you feel awful about yourself and it can play into suicidal thoughts. Especially, when every single other everyday task seems to require so much effort that your quality of life just crumbles and is reduced to nothing.

This is why learning about strategies to support clients with leaden paralysis is so important.

For people with depression, I hope you now have some strategies to help you get out of bed in the morning and I hope you realise that you aren't alone. What you're experiencing is normal for depression and it is a normal response for whatever is causing your difficulties and that's why talking to a mental health professional is critical.

Here are some questions at the end of this podcast episode:

- Have you ever encountered leaden paralysis before? Either through personal or clinical experience.
- How have you dealt with these experiences of leaden paralysis?
- Do you know how to practise self-kindness?
- How could you learn more about self-kindness?
- What would you say to a loved one and/ or client who struggles to get out of bed in the morning because of their depression?

Clinical Psychology References and Further Reading

Alshehri, T., Mook-Kanamori, D. O., de Mutsert, R., Penninx, B. W., Rosendaal, F. R., le Cessie, S., & Milaneschi, Y. (2023). The association between adiposity and atypical energy-related symptoms of depression: a role for metabolic dysregulations. *Brain, Behavior, and Immunity*, *108*, 197-203.

Chae, W. R., Baumert, J., Nübel, J., Brasanac, J., Gold, S. M., Hapke, U., & Otte, C. (2023). Associations between individual depressive symptoms and immunometabolic characteristics in major depression. *European Neuropsychopharmacology*, *71*, 25-40.

Collins, K. A., Eng, G. K., Tural, Ü., Irvin, M. K., Iosifescu, D. V., & Stern, E. R. (2022). Affective and somatic symptom clusters in depression and their relationship to treatment outcomes in the STAR* D sample. *Journal of Affective Disorders*, *300*, 469-473.

Friedrich, M. J. (2017). Depression is the leading cause of disability around the world. Jama, 317(15), 1517-1517.

Guo, Z. P., Chen, L., Tang, L. R., Gao, Y., Qu, M., Wang, L., & Liu, C. H. (2025). The differential orbitofrontal activity and connectivity between atypical and typical major depressive disorder. *NeuroImage: Clinical*, *45*, 103717.

https://www.psychologytoday.com/us/blog/beyond-mental-health/202407/when-it-feels-impossible-to-get-out-of-bed

Qi, B., MacDonald, K., Berlim, M. T., Fielding, A., Lis, E., Low, N., ... & Trakadis, Y.

(2020). Balance problems, paralysis, and angina as clinical markers for severity in major depression. Frontiers in psychiatry, 11, 567394.

Vreijling, S. R., Fatt, C. R. C., Williams, L. M., Schatzberg, A. F., Usherwood, T., Nemeroff, C. B., ... & Lamers, F. (2024). Features of immunometabolic depression as predictors of antidepressant treatment outcomes: pooled analysis of four clinical trials. *The British Journal of Psychiatry*, *224*(3), 89-97.

ARE INFANTS MORAL?

If you've been listening to The Psychology World Podcast for a while then you might have noticed that from time to time I report on research concerning the morality of infants. I've always found it is interesting and I like how research is starting to recognise that infants can be naturally moral. And yet this challenges a lot of traditional theories that have a lot of research support. Resulting in a rather large paradox for researchers. In this developmental psychology episode, you'll learn are infants moral by learning about a range of social and developmental factors that help to make infants moral (and immoral too). If you like learning about morality, prosocial behaviour and child psychology then you'll enjoy today's episode.

Are Infants Moral?

When it comes to the topic of morality in children and more specifically infants, there are generally two schools of thought. Firstly, you have the more traditional school of thought that has a lot of research support and this is the idea that children learn their morality through their parents. There are a lot of references in the Reference section at the bottom of the podcast episode, but one piece of evidence for this theory is how morality varies from culture to culture. This supports the social explanation of morality, because if morality was innate then morality wouldn't vary as much from culture to culture because our sense of morality would have evolved as part of our species.

Then another school of thought that has a growing body of evidence comes from researchers like Yale Professor Karen Wyn. These researchers propose morality begins in infancy and this runs against the idea that morality is taught through parents.

How can there be so much evidence for our theories?

Could it be because they are both right?

There are a few different reasons about why Wyn and her critics are both right about morality and how it develops. Firstly, they're both right because the definition of morality varies slightly from study to study as does the level or measures of behaviour each study looks at. Since Wyn's research refers to an infant's innate propensity to be prosocial, whilst her critics focus on social conventions that differ from place to place.

I know this little example is silly in the grand scheme of things, but it is very apt here. In the UK, it isn't considered moral or immoral to put salt and pepper on your food, but in Portugal, it is considered rude and by extension, immoral to put extra salt and pepper on your food. Since you are implying the chef hasn't seasoned their food right.

As a result, it is possible that morality is an innate human trait that is universal in the human species but it is implemented and expressed differently between cultures and even from person to person. We only need to think about the different behaviours people think are moral within a single country or town, let alone an entire species.

What Did Wyn's Research Show?

In addition, Wyn found through her series of experiments that infants look longer at helping puppets than puppets that stopped another puppet from opening a box. As well as different variations of the experiment found the exact same thing, so this suggests infants prefer people who help others compared to people who made things more difficult for other people.

Of course, this research is only suggestive at this point in time, but what makes it interesting is that Wyn's study is part of a growing body of research making the same point. Infants do offer help, they do comfort people in distress and they prefer people who do the same.

Personally, I think this is actually a rather lovely and even heartwarming finding. Especially, because people like me who focus so much on clinical psychology, we read and focus on mental health conditions, mental health difficulties and the "darker" side of human behaviour from time to time. Therefore, this study is a pleasant reminder about the lighter side of human behaviour and how great psychology research can be.

Can These Prosocial Tendencies Be Overwritten?

Unfortunately, as you can probably guess, the innate sense of morality in an infant doesn't stay with an infant unless a parent builds on these propensities. Yet this isn't always just down to the parent, because these prosocial propensities can be overridden by peers and the larger culture as a whole if they convey very different values.

What Did Wyn Find Out About Prejudice?

An interesting finding of Wyn's study is that she found another trait that impacted the infant's judgements and this certainly isn't positive if you really think about it. So Wyn found that infants preferred the puppets who liked the same food as the infant. On the surface, this is a very normal finding that I wouldn't have cared less about, but Wyn makes a very interesting point that I can definitely understand.

She implied that this could be the root adult of prejudice because infants show we might prefer people who are like us and dislike people who are not like us. Remember, the babies also liked the puppets that were like them in terms of they shared similar interests in food, and at first, I thought this sounded like a silly example. But how many conversations as adults have all of us started and bonded over because of food?

A lot, so I think this food preference does hold ecological validity because it continues into adulthood. It was only a few days ago that me and a friend were having a conversation about nachos, and neither one of us are children.

Wyn talks about this finding more with the following quote:

"Babies and infants were far more likely to approve of the similar puppets being helped, while having the same positive reaction when the puppets that chose different foods were hindered," Wynn said. "This reaction seems to suggest the roots of the adult impulses toward xenophobia, prejudice and war."

I think this is a very interesting point that will hopefully be researched more in the future.

Conclusion

Overall, at the end of this podcast episode, we know that infants have an innate sense of morality and what is morally right and wrong. Yet infants have a sense of "us and them" as well and this is important to realise when it comes to morality, because morality does account for in-group cohesion and this is something I'll talk more about in the future. And yet, morality and "us and them" thinking accounts for the violence that is found in religion as well according to the Philosopher John Teehan.

Therefore, I think the biggest takeaway from today's episode is to foster that sense of love, compassion and morality in our infants. We need to raise them to be moral, be kind and to be compassionate to other people, because that will help to make the world a better and safer place for everyone.

And isn't that the world we want to live in?

Social Psychology References

Bloom, P. (2010). The moral life of babies. *New York Times Magazine*, *3*, MM44.

Bloom, P., & Wynn, K. (2016). What develops in moral development. *Core knowledge and conceptual change*, 347-364.

Dahl, A. (2014). Definitions and Developmental Processes in Research on Infant MoralityCommentary on Tafreshi, Thompson, and Racine. *Human Development*, *57*(4), 241-249.

Hamlin, J. K. (2015). Does the infant possess a moral concept?.

Hamlin, J. K., & Wynn, K. (2011). Young infants prefer prosocial to antisocial others. *Cognitive development*, *26*(1), 30-39.

Hamlin, J. K., Mahajan, N., Liberman, Z., & Wynn, K. (2013). Not like me= bad: Infants prefer those who harm dissimilar others. *Psychological science*, *24*(4), 589-594.

Hamlin, J. K., Wynn, K., Bloom, P., & Mahajan, N. (2011). How infants and toddlers react to antisocial others. *Proceedings of the national academy of sciences*, *108*(50), 19931-19936.

Marshall, J., Wynn, K., & Bloom, P. (2020). Do children and adults take social relationship into account when evaluating people's actions?. *Child Development*, *91*(5), e1082-e1100.

Sheskin, M., Bloom, P., & Wynn, K. (2014). Anti-equality: Social comparison in young children. *Cognition*, *130*(2), 152-156.

Whiteley, C. (2022) Psychology of Relationships: The Social Psychology of Friendships, Romantic Relationships and More. CGD Publishing. England.

Wynn, K., & Bloom, P. (2014). The moral baby. In M. Killen & J. G. Smetana (Eds.), *Handbook of moral development* (2nd ed., pp. 435–453). Psychology Press.

Wynn, K., Bloom, P., Jordan, A., Marshall, J., & Sheskin, M. (2018). Not noble savages after all: Limits to early altruism. *Current Directions in Psychological Science*, *27*(1), 3-8.

WHAT IS SOCIAL PRESCRIBING?

Recently, as I continue to search for a mental health-related job to do after my clinical psychology MSc, I came across a job for a Social Prescriber Line Worker. I applied for the job, I got an interview but I have little idea what a social prescriber actually does. Chances are, you don't either because this is a very new job role in the United Kingdom's National Health Service, but it serves a very interesting, unique and important role in modern mental healthcare. Therefore, in this clinical psychology podcast episode, you'll learn what is social prescribing, how does social prescribing fit within the larger mental health job market and how can social prescribing improve lives. If you enjoy learning about mental health, careers in psychology and multidisciplinary approaches to therapy. Then this is a brilliant episode for you.

What Is Social Prescribing?

Social prescribing, according to the NHS, is a major part of Universal Personalised Care and this is an approach to mental health that seeks to connect people to services, groups and activities in their community. These activities seek to meet the social, emotional as well as practical needs of the person to improve their health and wellbeing.

In addition, social prescribing isn't limited to one clinical population or one age group. Instead social prescribing is an all-age, whole population approach to healthcare that can work even better for people who are lonely or isolated, they have complex social needs that might impact their mental health, they need support with low-level mental health difficulties and they have one or more long-term conditions.

The person who does the social prescribing is called a social prescribing line worker and these Line Workers work for local agencies, like social care, local charities and health services. Also, these Line Workers give people time to focus on what matters to them so together the client and the Line Worker can co-produce a simple personalised care and support plan. As well as the Line Worker helps people to take control of their own health and wellbeing.

Personally, I flat out love this approach to mental healthcare so far, because it is built on the same reason why I love formulation. We are the experts in psychological theory and research, but the client is always the expert in themselves, their life and their lived experience. This is why we always need to work *with* the client to co-produce a care plan, so they feel empowered and like they can take back control. Especially, because in my experience, depression, anxiety and other mental health conditions steal that power from a person.

Coproducing care plans can help clients to get that sense of power back.

In addition, I really like how Line Workers mean we can reduce waiting lists because instead of clients with low level mental health difficulties being abandoned until their difficulties become severe enough that they need to be added to a waiting list for longer-term, more expensive psychological therapy, we can put them in touch with local services that might help improve their mental health and wellbeing. This is essentially another, less official version of behavioural activation. By helping someone with a mental health condition to take part in and do what they love then it can lead to positive mental health outcomes, to grossly oversimplify.

Line workers are a part of Primary Care Networks (PCNs) and the idea behind this is that it allows every person in England to access a social prescribing service through their General Practice.

Furthermore, social prescribing line workers support existing community groups to be sustainable as well as accessible for everyone. Equally, they help people to start new groups and line workers work with all local partners, so no one is left out. Essentially, I understand this mentality as a sort of "a rising tide lifts all boats" mentality. In other words if all social groups are thriving then everyone benefits in society.

<u>What Difference Does Social Prescribing Make?</u>

According to the NHS, there is a growing body of evidence showing the stark positive impact that social prescribing can have on individuals, like the report by Dayson and Batty (2020). Research shows that social prescribing gives people more control over their lives so this improves their mental health, as well as service evaluations show that social prescribing reduces pressure on NHS services. Such as, a reduction in A&E attendance, GP Consultations and hospital bed stays for people. As well as in 2017, the University of Westminster found that social prescribing leads to 28% fewer GP consultations and 24% fewer A&E visits.

It's clear that social prescribing does have a starkly positive impact on people and their mental health, and it has wider benefits for the National Health Service too.

What Makes A Good Social Prescribing Scheme?

Finally, a good social prescribing scheme is made up of support for community groups, a common outcomes framework, workforce development, easy referral from all local agencies, a co-produced personalised plan that is based on what matters to the client you're supporting as well as collaborative commissioning and partner working.

Also, social prescribing link workers are employed to give time to people to focus on what matters to them. These are the key factors that make a good social prescribing scheme.

Conclusion

Whilst social prescribing is a relatively new form of mental health support, I strongly believe that it's important for aspiring and qualified psychologists to be aware of. In case you're like me and you're close to finishing your time at university, you'll be looking for mental health-related jobs so we can get the practical work experience we need to be able to apply for the Doctorate of Clinical Psychology in a few years. Getting involved in social prescribing work might be a useful first step as we continue our psychology journey.

Just a thought.

What do you think?

Clinical Psychology References and Further Reading

Dayson, C., & Batty, E. (2020). Social prescribing and the value of small providers-evidence from the evaluation of the Rotherham social prescribing service.

Evers, S., Husk, K., Napierala, H., Wendt, L., & Gerhardus, A. (2024). Theories used to develop or evaluate social prescribing in studies: a scoping review. *BMC Health Services Research*, *24*(1), 140.

Haslam, S. A., Haslam, C., Cruwys, T., Sharman, L. S., Hayes, S., Walter, Z., ... & Young, T. (2024). Tackling loneliness together: A three-tier social identity framework for social prescribing. *Group Processes & Intergroup Relations*, *27*(5), 1128-1150.

https://www.england.nhs.uk/personalisedcare/comprehensive-model/

https://www.england.nhs.uk/personalisedcare/pcsp/

https://www.england.nhs.uk/personalisedcare/social-prescribing/faqs/

https://www.england.nhs.uk/personalisedcare/workforce-and-training/social-prescribing-link-workers/

https://www.england.nhs.uk/primary-care/primary-care-networks/

Sachs, A. L., Kolster, A., Wrigley, J., Papon, V., Opacin, N., Hill, N., ... & Litt, J. (2024). Connecting through nature: A systematic review of the effectiveness of nature-based social prescribing practices to combat loneliness. *Landscape and Urban Planning*, *248*, 105071.

Scarpetti, G., Shadowen, H., Williams, G. A., Winkelmann, J., Kroneman, M.,

Groenewegen, P. P., ... & van Ginneken, E. (2024). A comparison of social prescribing approaches across twelve high-income countries. *Health policy*, *142*, 104992.

BESTSELLING AUTHOR OF FORENSIC PSYCHOLOGY
CONNOR WHITELEY
FORENSIC PSYCHOLOGY OF TERRORISM AND HOSTAGE-TAKING
A FORENSIC AND CRIMINAL PSYCHOLOGY GUIDE TO UNDERSTANDING TERRORISTS, TERRORISM AND HOSTAGE SITUATIONS

FORENSIC PSYCHOLOGY OF TERRORISM AND HOSTAGE-TAKING

A Forensic and Criminal Psychology Guide to Understanding Terrorists, Terrorism and Hostage Situations

INTRODUCTION

Of all the extreme examples of criminal behaviour, like psychopaths, serial killers and more, there is one crime that creates so much interest and fascination that hundreds of myths and misconceptions get created to help people understand this most horrific example of criminal behaviour.

That is terrorism and hostage-taking.

Terrorism evokes, rightly, a lot of fear in people but a lot of interest and fascination as well. Since all of us are curious about what makes someone into a terrorist? Is it a combination of mental health or personality or social psychological factors?

This is what this book aims to investigate as we look into the forensic psychology research on terrorism. In this book, you'll learn about:

- What are the consequences of terrorism and why is it important to investigate?
- What makes a terrorist?
- How do people develop ideologies and mental processes supporting terror attacks?
- How do terror groups fall?
- And more.

If you want an engaging, easy-to-understand guide to terrorism and hostage-taking then you will love this book.

In addition, this book is for psychology students and professionals that want to understand the research on terrorism, including its limitations and the problem with terrorism research. All of this is explained in a fun, conversational tone that makes the material interesting and engaging.

Who Am I?

Personally, I always love to know who the author is of the nonfiction I read so I know the information is coming from a good source. In case you're like me, I'm Connor Whiteley, the internationally bestselling author of over 40 psychology books.

In addition, I am the host of *The Psychology World Podcast,* a weekly show exploring a new psychology topic each week and delivering the latest psychology news. Available on all major podcast apps and YouTube.

Finally, I am a psychology graduate studying a Clinical Psychology Masters at the University of Kent, England.

So now we know more about each other, let's dive into the great topic of terrorism and hostage-taking.

INTRODUCTION TO TERRORISM AND CONSEQUENCES OF TERRORISM

Before we explore a lot of great topics like what makes someone into a terrorist, what makes a suicide bomber and then we explore hostage situations, we need to understand why this is important at a larger scale first of all.

Therefore, terrorism is becoming of growing importance to governments over the past few decades because the public care about it and governments want to keep the public safe. For example, the UK's homeland security spend has increased from £1 billion in 2004 to £3 billion in 2009 (Mythen and Walklate, 2005) and it is estimated to be £3.5 billion in 2010/2011 (Secret Service, 2007). Therefore, as you can see governments are spending more and more on terrorism each year.

However, this is a little odd to some extent because terrorism actually doesn't kill that many people in the grand scheme of things.

Now please bear with me because I promise you there is a point here.

Since if we look at the United States of America, terrorism has killed at least 3,000 people in the decade of about 2005 to 2015, and the US spends about $0.5 billion on each death. Whereas stroke is the US's third largest killer and only $2,000 per death is spent (Sinn, 2017). You would have assumed that you would want to spend more on the larger killer, again there is a point explaining all of this later on.

Also, terrorism is low cost for the terrorist too because it only costs $150 to buy the materials needed for a suicide bomb large enough to kill 12 people on average (Lomborg, 2008).

What Are The Waves of Modern Terrorism?

When I first came across this research I was rather amazed because I do enjoy history and the history of terrorism and how it's evolved is certainly interesting and it helps to give the research we're going to be looking at a bit of a historical perspective to show how far terrorism has sadly come.

As a result, authors like Rapport (2004) and Post, McGinnis and Moody (2014) suggest there are 4 waves of modern terrorism. The first stage of modern terrorism started in 1880 with Anarchists in Russia spreading globally, and these anarchists used modern methods of communication effectively.

Secondly, the modern terrorism movement changed into the nationalist-anti-colonist movement between World War 1 and 2 where people sought to fulfil the mission of securing their nation's freedom from Imperial Masters.

Thirdly, modern terrorism morphed again into a social revolutionary wave that generally opposed the parent generation's ideals and this movement began in the 1960s. This sort of movement was frequently used in opposition against the Vietnam War. Like the weather man in USA or the shining path in Peru.

Fourthly, and this is a little more important for the current socio-political climate because we are sort of coming out of the end of this wave but a lot of the major terror events in the lives of you readers will be in this wave, modern terrorism changed in the 1980s to centre itself around religion. And this happened to a whole range of religions and this certainly wasn't just Islam. Then the use of social media highlights and supports the importance of communication that characterised modern terrorism according to Rapport.

Also, what's important to note about this fourth wave is that real fundamentalists employ mass destruction (Hudson, 1999) and this is something that seriously sets the fourth wave apart from previous waves of terrorism.

Since before this, terror groups had very different attitudes. For instance, before the fourth wave, terror groups like the IRA used to give specific warnings about their targets, now suicide is a weapon and tens can be killed instantly without warning.

Finally, in the past few years and a bit a new wave has been added by Post et al. (2014) and this is the Lone-Wolf wave. Which I find a little scary to be honest because before it was entire groups wanting to commit terror groups but now Lone-wolves can commit terror attacks unlike before. They can find blueprints online for 3D printing guns and bomb parts. They can go down the shop can find everything you need for a fertilizer bomb (okay you could always do that option), but you don't need to be an organised group anymore to commit a terrorist attack.

That was a cheery paragraph. Sorry, that is the darkest I personally go in this book.

However, as you can see in this section of the chapter, whenever there is novel advancement in technology, like the advent of social media or mobile phones or other forms of communication, the wave of terrorism morphs into a new and different form.

The Research Problem Of Terrorism

Something you might notice fairly quickly in this book is that in the later chapters we will focus a little more on research studies, and we'll all notice that there is a massive, massive research problem in the terrorism field. This book tries to include some of the "best" studies but to be honest, even that is pushing it.

Due to there has been a lot of research into terrorism done over the past 40 years but the problem is that the vast majority of this research lacks empirical rigour (Borum, 2004) so this means the findings and the conclusions are hardly convincing.

Then again, something else I mention through the rest of the book is I suppose we need to have empathy to some extent. Since research terrorism is not easy, not only from a legal perspective but also from a participant recruitment viewpoint. As well as many of the most basic research methodologies cannot be used in terrorism research for the same reasons. For instance, I would rather like to know how would you use a semi-structured interview design. It's basic but it still gives us problems because terrorists are very unlikely to sit down with you and tell you everything you want to know. I would also like to know where are you going to find enough terrorists that are willing to talk to give your study some power, and finally I would like to know how researchers would overcome the classic forensic psychology problem of us typically only having access to prisoners. Also known as terrorists that got caught. This automatically skews our research because we have no idea about the behaviour of terrorists that haven't been caught.

All classic problems in forensic psychology research but the field of terrorism amplifies them.

As a result, this has led the vast majority of publications on terrorism to be only speculative or full of conjecture. Again this is not science.

Overall, terrorism research is avoided by mainstream psychology because of all these problems, and instead this research area survives in the cracks and crevices between disciplines like politics, sociology and psychology (Silker, 2004).

What Is The Nature Of Terrorism And How Do Terrorists Attack?

Another problem with terrorism research is the definition of what is terrorism? Logically speaking and a common sense definition is something along the lines of, a group of people who plan and carry out acts of violence with a political motive.

However, even though this is a fairly basic definition, it is far from perfect. Since this definition makes it difficult to differentiate terrorism from other forms of violence. For example, the sort of violence that can erupt at a political rally. That is violence with a political motive, but I really wouldn't say it's terrorism.

Therefore, there are a lot of questions that make creating a definition of terrorism very difficult.

In addition, there are databases that collect information from substantial data sets concerning terrorist incidents. Like the International Terrorism: Attributes of Terrorist Events (ITATE). And I'm mentioning this because these databases as well as other advanced statistical methods (like non-metric multi-dimensional scaling) were used by Yokota, Fjytam, Watanabe and Wachi (2007) to identify patterns in terrorism.

These analyses allowed the researchers to code each terrorist incident with a number of different dimensions so they were able to find common links with various strengths to create clusters.

As a result, three attack strategies emerged. Firstly, there is the "threat" strategy where terror groups seek to intimidate people and society and the aim here isn't to cause casualties. Secondly, there is the "mean" strategy where the victims are used as a way of negotiating the goals of the terror group. Thirdly, there is the "violence" strategy where the groups of people or individuals are targeted to be injured or killed by the terror groups.

I was somewhat surprised to learn that the most common attack strategy isn't violence, it is actually "threat" because 87% of terrorist organisations had over 50% of their incidents in that one group. Consequently, we can see that terrorist organisations don't stick to one strategy and it can vary so the researchers suggested that this small amount of variation could be a result of the instability within these terrorist organisations.

<u>What Are The Consequences Of Terrorism?</u>

Now this section really helps to put the rest of the book into perspective because it shows dealing with and understanding terrorism is beyond critical. The reason for this is because in society there is a general idea that the general public are extremely resilient against terrorism and it is because of this resilience that terrorism has minimal effect on the general public.

This is a lie society creates for itself obviously.

I say this because there's a lot of research showing that terrorism has profound effects on the general public. For example, DiMaggio and Galea (2006) show us results from a meta-analysis on the aftermath of terrorist incidents like 9/11 and the 2005 London Tube and bus bombings. Their results show that the rate of Post-Traumatic Stress Disorder for people were directly affected by the terrorism was between 12% to 16%. This shows us that being directly affected by a terrorist incident leads to the development of mental health conditions.

Another example can be seen in Gabriel et al. (2007) but for historical context, on the 11th March 2004 in Spain bombs exploded on 4 early commuter trains resulting in 400 people being taken to hospital and 200 people died, so Gabriel et al. (2007) wanted to study the aftermath on 3 different groups. The people injured in the blast, the people in the neighbourhood of the victims but didn't know them, and the final group was the police officers involved in the rescue.

The researchers interviewed members of each group on a one-on-one basis within 3 months and then the researchers used standard diagnostic instruments like the mini-international neuropsychiatric interview and Davidson Trauma Scale to assess the mental health of participants.

Their results showed the injured group had the most evidence of current mental health conditions with 58% of them meeting a criteria for diagnosis. Then 26% of the local area group had the criteria and then only 4% of the police officers did. The most common mental health condition was PTSD at 44%.

And what was really interesting about this data was the sheer amount of comorbidity because 53% of the injured group showed comorbidity compared to 22% of the local area group.

Therefore, compared to the last study we looked at, this gives us clearer results on the impact of direct victimisation on victims but also secondary victimisation too. Since if secondary victimisation wasn't an outcome of terrorism then the local group should have seen results like the police officers, but it is clear the people in the neighbourhoods of the victims were profoundly affected by the terrorist attack.

Additionally, DiMaggio, Galea and Richardson (2007) found that 9/11 caused an increase of mental health admissions to hospitals and the closer you were to the attack, the likelihood of you developing a mental health condition increased.

As well as Jhangiani (2010) reviewed 18 studies into psychological consequences of the 9/11 attack and their results showed evidence of people experiencing poorer mental health after the New York and Washington D.C attacks. Although, the review did show that people's mental health returned to pre-attack levels quickly about 6 months after the attacks, or some studies suggested it was better soon after the attack.

The precise details of this improvement vary case to case but the negative mental health outcomes of terrorist attacks aren't permeant.

Also, the effects of a terrorist attack were worse if a person had a history of mental health conditions beforehand, if they knew someone involved like a victim, if they were physically very close to the attack but if they were outside the attack area they experienced a more minimal effect of the attack.

Overall, whilst positive responses to terror attacks were useful in the long-term in increasing helping behaviour and even increase life satisfaction, this chapter so far has still shown us the deadly and foul consequences that terrorist attacks have on society. Especially, when we consider that all of us can be considered victims of terrorist attacks directly or indirectly because of primary and secondary victimisation.

What Affects Our Response To Attacks?

Speaking of positive responses to terrorist attacks, let's see what impacts our responses. Ferguson and Kamble (2012) studied the responses of UK and Indian students to the Mukai terrorist attacks of 2008. These terrorist attacks involved a series of bombing with a minimum of 173 dead and lots more injured and these researchers decided to examine the effect of the Just World Beliefs (Lerner, 1980) on helping responses. And in case you're unfamiliar with Just World Beliefs, the short answer is that if people believe in Just World Beliefs then they believe that you get what you deserve in life. For example, if you're a victim of a terrorist attack then you're getting your just desserts for some wrong you have previously done.

The reason why these researchers choose to study Just World Beliefs is because when dreadful events happen these aren't easily reconciled with these Just World Beliefs, because at first people with Just World Beliefs want to help others but they can also blame victims for their poor character or responsibilities.

Therefore, Ferguson and Kamble boiled it down to people believing we get what we deserve and get what's coming to us.

However, the results surprised the researchers a lot because the participants completed the Global Beliefs in Just World Scale (Lipkus, 1991) and (remember this was a terrorist attack against India) and the results showed Indian students had more Just World beliefs than UK students. Now this could be down to cultural differences and Indian students had higher levels of terrorism-related distress, more desire for revenge and higher levels of terrorism denial. Regardless of the Just World Belief, those higher in Just World Beliefs tended to have higher levels of a desire for revenge and terrorism denial.

The researchers concluded that these findings suggest this shows multiple strategies are used to maintain belief in a Just World. Which makes sense when we consider that Just World Beliefs can be used to improve someone's self-esteem and other psychological benefits because it helps them to feel that the world isn't chaotic and it's a safe place.

Overall, at the end of this chapter, we can conclude that the public's response to terrorist attacks are complex judging from the available research, and systemic research into terrorism is difficult because it is difficult to plan and has to be done quickly. Also, this makes it hard to be systematic and theoretical in orientation compared to being pragmatic about the aims of study.

In addition, if we go back to what I say at the very beginning of the chapter, there is a reason why governments spend so much money on anti-terrorism because whilst the research generally accepts that terrorists seek to scare the public to put pressure on governments to comply with them, in reality governments don't seek to reduce this fear but to maintain it at a high level (Braithwaite, 2013). Since Braithwaite suggests this could be to avoid the government being blamed for saying the public are safe when they're not. But this could be because this level of fear makes the public alert so they report things that suggest an attack is coming.

Personally, I was rather shocked when I first read that but it makes sense and in the grand scheme f things, I would much rather have a base level of fear and be alert for terrorist activity then think the world was extremely safe, only to be the victim of a terror attack.

So after this great introduction to terrorism, are there any personality or mental health factors that could make someone into a terrorist?

IS THERE A TERRORIST PERSONALITY OR MENTAL HEALTH CONDITION? AND SUICIDE BOMBERS

Now I absolutely have to admit I flat out cringe whenever I see academics or psychology students talking about a "terrorist or criminal personality" or whether a mental health condition has led to a particular behaviour. I tend to cringe because as you'll find out about in this chapter, it is extremely, extremely unlikely that a personality trait or a mental health condition will lead someone to become a terrorist or a criminal.

I think the only real reason why these debates happen in the first place is because these debate pop up in mainstream culture from the media, politicians and different conversations between friends and family. Then academics want to test out the idea, and to be honest, I might be being a little critical here but we do need to rule out these personality and mental health factors so it is good that this research has been conducted.

Although, because my background is in

clinical psychology, I want to say upfront here that I will not be using the terms psychopathology or mental disorder or mental illness in this book unless a paper has specifically used it and I want to reuse it for a reason. This is because modern clinical psychology understands how blaming, judgmental and unhelpful these terms are. Since mental health conditions, like depression and anxiety, are a part of a person and they cannot be cured. They don't mean anything is wrong with a person. And instead, it is our job as current or future clinical psychologists to help people improve their coping mechanisms so they can live full lives.

Anyway, that's me done on my soapbox.

Therefore, in this chapter, we'll be exploring some of this research before we move onto talking about suicide bombers.

Is There A Terrorist Personality?

One of the main reasons in academia why this personality strain of research has popped up is because extremists are very hard to conceptualise. Since are they all mad (I hate that term)? Are they all strong? Are they all suicide prone?

On the whole, it is very tempting to label terrorist actions as insane and the result of some personality factor or mental health condition. Yet this is very unhelpful for the clinical populations that actually have mental health conditions as this perpetuates and creates stigma that shouldn't be there in the first place.

Moreover, it is dangerous to label certain actions as one thing when the truth is a lot, lot more complex than that given label. For example, the media feeds laypeople the idea that all suicide bombers are religious zealots but this isn't true in the slightest. Since the Tami tigers of Sri Lanka are political suicide bombers with operations all over the world.

Another false assumption is that it is the male sex that exclusively performs suicide bombings, but there are a surprising amount of women that partake in these terrorism acts. For example, the Tami Tigers of Sri Lanka and Kurdistan Workers party use women bombers as much as men (Ergil, 2001).

Consequently, it isn't empirically correct at all to say that suicide bombers are simply religious extremists.

Overall, there is remarkable consensus that that there is no terrorist personality (Silk, 2004) and stressing and having conversations about there being no mental abnormality is also important when dealing with terrorists.

One academic that tries to explain this is Borum (2004, 2014) because this researcher summarised the literature saying that terrorism is poorly explained by psychopathology. And of course, some terrorism will be explained by mental health conditions, but far from all of it is.

What About A Terrorist Profile?

As someone who wrote a bestselling *Criminal Profiling* book that explores the truth about how horrifically bad criminal profiling is, this makes me laugh because any sort of "profiles" are just setting up researchers to fail. Because guess what? Humans are all different so they can't be accurately profiled.

Anyway, this is a real shocker but there are no useful constructed profiles of terrorists. Since Maghan (1998) explained that terrorists cover all types of people from the self-doubting wreck to those haunted by their personal demons, but madness or mental disorders have no role to play as an explanatory concept for why someone becomes a terrorist.

This is supported by Ruby (2002) as well who commented terrorists are rational, lucid people, with Silke (1998) supporting this finding too. As well as Ariel Merari at the university of Tel Avia studied 32 suicide bombers and she found no evidence of suicidality or social dysfunction which would account for their actions.

Again, even more evidence that terrorism isn't caused by mental health conditions.

One of the reasons for these findings is because terror groups take advantage of new recruits having religious fanaticism and nationalism instead of mental health conditions, but even this nationalism and fanaticism fails to account for why some people and not others become suicide bombers.

As a result, Merari and other researchers argue that terrorists are normal people who are a cross-section of society with there being no significant evidence of mental health conditions amongst them.

What About Terrorism And Psychopathy?

It's still understandable though why people think there is a link between mental health and terrorism, because the vast majority of terrorist acts are atrocities and difficult for people to understand. For example, the humiliation of hostages and the slow videotaped beheadings of them led to questions of psychopathy. Another reason why this is understandable is because we know that psychopaths commit some horrific and strange murders.

Leading some researchers to review this assumption and one such researcher was Borum (2004) who found that psychopaths aren't good fits for any organisation (in slight contradiction to other studies) because whilst selflessness and dedication might be required of terrorists, these two major characteristics are extremely, extremely different to the characteristics showed by psychopaths.

Therefore, I think after all these studies, all these different aspects of mental health and personality factors, we can confirm that someone doesn't become a terrorist because of a mental health condition or personality factors. Or at least the vast, vast majority of them do not.

If It Isn't Caused By Mental Health Conditions Or Personality Factors Why Do People Become Terrorists?

Whilst we talk about this again in the next chapter, we can draw on social psychology research to explain this because the subdiscipline shows how good people can do bad things as part of normal social processes. I think everyone reading this book is familiar with good old Milgram and his 1974 study where he showed that obedience is a powerful force and can make university students electrocute someone pass the point of death. Then a lot of other research that looked into why different things happened in World War two proves the same point.

In addition, one of my favourite little references I've discovered in the course of my research for this book was made by Taylor and Quayle (1994) because they asked the very simple question of we don't expect all university students to be the same or even similar, so why do we expect terrorists to be the same?

It's a good point and this is why I flat out

hate "profiling" and any sort of research that investigates the profiles of certain people. These researchers are always setting themselves up for failure.

As a result, Borum (2014) suggested the study of terrorism might progress faster if the field adopts more complex models of how people's psychology involving normal mental states and processes might explain why a person might become involves in terrorist activity.

Here Borum acknowledges that there is contextual and environmental factors going on here because terrorism is more common in some settings compared to others, and a person's worldview (which is different to personality) is important in them becoming a terrorist too. For example, the 4 Borum mentioned is Authoritarianism, dogmatism, fundamentalism and apocalypticism.

Now authoritarianism is important in terrorism research (and basically everything social psychology looks at) because this is a learnt attitude about being hostile and aggressive towards outgroups and submissiveness towards authority figures as well as being conservative. This is useful to terrorism because it means the person is more likely to take part in aggressive and hostile acts towards outgroups whilst being submissive and following orders from the leadership.

Similar to authoritarianism, dogmatism needs to be looked at here because a dogmatic person manifests a very closed set of strongly held beliefs and disbeliefs that are resistant to change. For example, any beliefs about how evil outgroups are and why they all need to be cleansed in fire. As well as dogmatic people need authority as absolute and are generally intolerant of most other people.

Whereas fundamentalist thinking involves a person having absolutist religious thinking about right and wrong and how people are categorised morally. In other words, whatever their religion says about a person that is it and they aren't going to change their minds about it. also, paranoia is a characteristic of fundamentalists as well as they rage against those who they believe have humiliated them. In terms of leadership this group of people are led by a charismatic leader who has intense conviction.

Then finally, apocalypticism is an aspect of fundamentalism and involves the belief of a future catastrophic event with only a few people having been warned of the event so they can be the most prepared for it and survive.

In addition, Borum suggests there is more to a person becoming involved in terrorism than personality and mental health factors. For example, the number of psychological vulnerabilities and number of propensities they have for terrorist activity. This is similar to how people get involved in cults as I talk about in my book, *Cult Psychology*.

As a result, terror groups can take advantage of these psychological vulnerabilities and make them have a role in "shaping" a person's thoughts and actions that can lead to an increased risk of getting involved with terrorism.

These psychological vulnerabilities can include, a person's need to belong, their need for meaning and identity as well as a person's perception of injustice and humiliation. All these are risk factors for terrorism because belonging to a terror group fulfils a lot of these needs for different people. Such as a terror group could provide someone with a chance to rectify the perceived injustice and humiliation, it gives them a family and something to belong to and it could give them a sense of meaning and purpose in their lives that helps to make up their identity.

Therefore, it isn't hard to see how an injustice or humiliation, like living under an occupying army, could push someone towards terrorism.

Also, it's important to consider how a person's motivational, attributional, attitudinal and volitional propensities of various types could also play a role in whether or not they become involved in terrorism. For example, the hostile attribution bias is the tendency to see hostility in what others say or do so it isn't hard to see how this links to terrorism. As people inclined towards terrorism might see an outgroup as speaking in a threatening way towards them in a preparation of an attack so terrorism might be a way for the person to strike first or something like that.

Overall, the entire point of this chapter so far has been to show that the psychology of terrorism research doesn't need to focus on mental health conditions as an explanation and instead this research area can be directed towards more ordinary psychological processes.

Suicidal Characteristics And Suicide Terrorism

I preluded to and briefly spoke about suicide bombers earlier in the chapter but now we need to focus on them a little more. Since suicide bombers are relatively rare in terrorism but they account for a high proportion of terrorism-related deaths.

And this is such an important thing to say that I have to say it upfront. We CANNOT regard suicide bombers as suicidal people because this flat out isn't how suicide bombers think, act or feel. Since Silke (2003) found that suicide bombers don't share the characteristics and motivations of typical people who want to commit suicide. As well as if you want to learn more about the psychology behind suicide, please check out *Suicide Psychology* for more information.

In addition, suicide bombers are actually psychologically stable people and they have very ordinary personalities when judged within their own culture. Meaning yet again, terrorists aren't mad or insane and terrorism cannot be explained by personality factors.

Also, the families of suicide bombers regard their relative's actions as positive and heroic. This and more is supported by Townsend (2007)'s views on the question of if suicide bombers are suicidal. Due to this is technically difficult to answer because the strategy was to assess the similarities and differences between what we know from suicide research as a whole and what we know from research on potential suicide bombers.

However, that is the first reason why this is a technically difficult question because we cannot conduct research on people who have successfully (I seriously hate that word) committed suicide and suicide bombers, because they are dead. Therefore, we can only conduct research on potential suicide bombers because these people never actually carried out the attack, thankfully.

Nonetheless, the research has shown that there is little correlation between suicidal people and suicide bombers and there are no typical range of motivations that link the two together.

In fact, mental health is a lot higher in the suicide bomber group because suicide bombers tend to have feelings of martyrdom and other positive feelings and in the service of Allah. As well as this type of Martyrdom is known as Istishahad (Abdel-Khalek, 2004).

This is important to bear in mind because suicide is not acceptable at all in Islam (and that alone has extremely damaging mental health implications for everyone in society but that is way beyond the scope of this book, but I talk more about that *Suicide Psychology*).

Furthermore, another interesting mismatch between suicide research and suicide bomber research is that there is some research that shows being religious is a protective factor against suicide (Nonemaker, McNelly and Blum, 2003). This further explains why suicide bombers aren't suicidal.

Also, whilst suicidal people might be motivated by their desire to end their pain and stop being a burden on the world (even though they are more loved than they'll ever know and life gets better), suicide bombers are motivated by vengeance. As well as suicidal people rarely feel vengeance and even then they don't want to harm others before their suicide.

However, there is at least one study that shows this isn't always the case because Merari, Diamont, Bibi, Broshi and Zakin (2010) found that 53% of suicide bombers had depressive and suicidal symptoms compared to only 21% of suicide bombing organisers and 8% of non-suicide bomber insurgents. Also, exclusive to suicide bombers was 40% showed suicidal tendencies that were not associated in their desire for martyrdom.

These are some interesting findings because they show that a small majority of suicide bombers could have their actions explained away by mental health conditions. But what about the remaining 47%, that is a massive amount of suicide bombings that aren't explained by mental health.

In response to that study, these results were strongly criticised by Bryon and Araj (2012) who suggested that these differences were not statistically significant and the judgement of the symptoms could have been wishful thinking on the part of researchers.

To support their argument, Bryon and Araj (2012) used evidence from a study of the Palestinian family and close friends of suicide bombers. And this study tell very different stories to Merari et al.'s because 76% of the suicide bombers showed no signs of depression or of personal crisis as far as the close friends or family knew.

As well as in the other 24%, the depression could have been down to political or social factors. And whatever the answer, depression rates for Palestinians living in Gaza or the West Bank was much the same.

The Need For Risk Assessments

To finish up this chapter, we need to talk about risk assessments for terrorists because how we actually go about rehabilitating terrorists has become a very practical and important concern for governments in recent years.

And before I continue, please allow me to jump on my little soapbox again. Rehabilitation works, there is a lot of psychological research showing that offenders that have been rehabilitated are much less likely to reoffend. That means these rehabilitated offenders are much less likely to commit crimes, have to go through the criminal justice system which costs taxpayer money and they don't need to go to prison which costs a lot of taxpayer money. So I know I am probably talking to the choir here but please don't dismiss the amazing power of rehabilitating criminals just because your local politician says it shouldn't be done. Please, read the research and then make an informed decision.

Anyway, Horgan and Bradlock (2010) reviewed a number of de-radicalisation programmes, and the researchers found that with terrorists having a lack of mental health conditions and us assuming that terrorists are psychologically normal. This presents psychologists with a massive problem because to have prisoners released from prison, a risk assessment needs to be done. But how do you carry out a risk assessment and determine the risk to the general public against future terrorist activity if they're psychologically normal and have no mental health conditions. There is basically no "warning signs" to look out for.

In addition, it's worth noting here that normally risk assessments work brilliantly and they do their job. But we don't know at this point in time how well these risk assessment apply to terrorists because these risk assessments are based on other non-terrorist prisoners and psychiatric patients.

Terrorists have nothing in common with either group as we've discussed in this chapter.

Moreover, Dernevick, Beck and Grams, Hogue and McGuire (2009a) argued that psychologists and psychiatrists don't have the knowledge base to formulate risk assessments for terrorists, because the current approaches, like risk to the public and chance of reoffending, cannot be applied to terrorists. Mainly because terrorist violence is so different to "normal" interpersonal violence.

Also, Dernevick et al. (2009a) were particularly concerned about the value of psychometric tests as these tests were developed on very different groups of offenders to terrorists. As well as there are other problems in establishing this risk assessment methodology. For example, the researchers pointed out how different groups of terrorists come from different routes. This can be seen in the last chapter when we were talking about the 5 waves of terrorism, all of those people came from extremely different routes depending on the wave they belonged too. And even though to be honest there's likely to be hundreds of different routes within each other.

As a result, we cannot think of terrorists as reoffending criminals as showed by Sagiman (2004) who showed that members of the worldwide fundamentalist network that Al-Qaeda is a part of, have no criminal history besides a couple of very small minor offences. He found that these members had no mental health conditions according to the DSM-4 as well.

On the whole, this means that the lack of a criminal history cannot be used to predict reoffending in terrorists, because the current method would say once they're released they present a very low risk to the public because they have no criminal history.

We don't know if this "very low" risk is true or false or extremely false at this point in time.

Interestingly, Gudjonsson (2009) regarded Dernevick et al. (2009a) somewhat negatively. As they responded by saying that some motivations of the terrorism might have changed or been removed by the time the terrorist is released from prison due to the political and motivational changes that might occur. For example, there's no research done on this at the moment at the time of writing, but the West's withdrawal from Afghanistan might be an example of this. It might be possible that the West's withdrawal might mean some terrorists might leave the organisation as they might perceive that the goals of their terror group have been achieved.

I don't know but it is just a thought and a question that I hope future research addresses.

One of the few recommendations about risk assessment for terrorists has been looking into the possible terrorist support network that a person might be able to plug themselves back into to once they're released. The idea here being if a prisoner cannot get back in contact with their terrorist network then they might not reoffend. This isn't traditionally done in risk assessments but I think this is going to have to be done in terrorism cases.

Although, I have to admit there is still a problem with this approach because of the 5th wave of terrorism. With lone-wolf terrorism becoming the new thing, I doubt a person would need a terrorist network to reoffend and become a very active terrorist once again.

WHAT MAKES A TERRORIST?

If a terrorist isn't made by personality factors or mental health conditions, then how does a person become a terrorist? This is the focus of this chapter and something we'll be exploring in a lot of depth.

The general consensus is that it takes time to convert a vulnerable person into a terrorist (Luckabaugh et al., 1997) because this is a process and different terrorist recruits have different motivations. For example, a need to belong, the development of a satisfactory personal identity, social alienation and boredom leads to dissidence and protests on a small scale, then over time terrorism, as well as histories of child abuse, trauma, humiliation and social injustice are common in a terrorist's background as well.

Although, Borum (2004) doesn't feel like this is helpful in explaining terrorism, because these factors are vulnerabilities and they don't make someone a terrorist on their own. Also, Merari (2007) may be suggesting general vulnerability factors when he suspects susceptibility to indoctrination is key to understanding suicide bombers. Due to most of the suicide bombers Merari studied where young and unattached people which are perfect types for all sorts of violent organisations.

As a result, Merari believed suicide terrorism could be understood as consequences of a terrorist system, with people being recruited through interpersonal connections that then supported the recruit all the way through to becoming a suicide bomber.

This is important to learn about because highly committed members of an organisation will spend hours talking to recruits, promoting the idea of martyrdom as will of the God and they focus on the illustrious past of Islam. Then the recruits become enmeshed in the group contact that is designed to help the recruit prove their allegiance to the organisation. Afterwards this "formal contract" creates a final personal commitment before a suicide bomber attack.

In addition, Merari compared terror groups to suicide bomb production lines using empirical support from Palestinian suicide bombers.

The stages of these production lines according to Merari include indoctrination. This is where members of terror groups with high authority constantly indoctrinate potential bombers to maintain their motivation to engage in the terrorist act and to prevent them changing their mind.

For Palestinian indoctrination, the themes were nationalism. For instance, Israel's humiliation of the Palestinian state and religious guarantees, by saying things like the suicide bomber will go to paradise after committing this act. As well as getting the recruit to commit to the group is done too at this stage where any doubts about committing to the attack are dealt with and the motivation for the attack is increased to maximum levels, or "maxed out" to use more urban slang terms.

Then the last stage is personal commitment and this can take the form of video recordings were the terrorist describes their intent to do the suicide bombing. This is partly done for their family, but it is also done as a way of getting irreversible commitment. As well as the bomber prepares farewell letters for friends and family too for later giving.

Also, at this point in the production line, Merari points out these would-be bombers are called "Living-Martyr", and this whole approach is sympathetic with Horgan and Taylor (2001)'s view that terrorists don't actively choose to become terrorists.

Instead becoming a terrorist is a gradual process where a potential terrorist is socialised with the recruiters having the ultimate goal of making them preform a terrorist act.

Of course, this is a process and not an absolute. People can leave the process at any point and this is to be expected given the high turnover rate in terrorist group membership (Crenshaw, 1986).

Moreover, Taylor and Louis (2004) suggested young people find themselves wanting a hopeful future and they engage in meaningful behaviour that helps them get ahead and will be satisfied with their life. Also, these young people's objective circumstances include no opportunity for a good future or advancement, and whilst they might find some collective identity in religions, living in a poor state and community makes them feel marginalised and lost without a clear group.

So it's easy to think how terror acts are result of group processes with Taylor (2010) asking can terrorism truly be understood as a phenomenon of group behaviour. Since Taylor (2010) distinctives between getting involved in a terror group and actually carrying out attacks.

Since group processes could be important as a backdrop in terrorism when cultural, political and social factors have a role to play. But these group processes fail to explain the act or episode of terrorism itself.

Taylor suggests there are two main issues with the "terrorism as group processes" argument. There is a lack of a good definition of what is terrorism besides from what terrorists do, and there isn't a clear idea of what is meant by group processes in relation to terrorism. Since there are times when group processes seem to play no or little role in a terrorist attack. Lone-wolf attacks spring to mind here.

Another extreme example is the reclusive Theodore John Kaczynski who's terrorist campaign lasted for 17 years with 12 bombs and 3 deaths for his environmental agenda that he largely made-up alone without a group behind him.

What Are Life Story Studies?

I do enjoy qualitative research and I think given how hard terrorism is to research, qualitative research methodologies might be useful. Of course, you will still have a lot of the same problems as the rest of terrorism research as I wrote about in the first chapter but qualitive research can still be useful.

Especially as Borum (2004) argued that a terrorist's life experience includes common themes. He suggests that these common themes aren't sufficient causes of terrorism, but they might be helpful to researchers to identify people susceptibility to being influenced by terrorist groups.

In some ways this argument fits with the narrative studies being done with terrorists because they reveal other factors are needed to understand what turns someone into a terrorist and it helps to show that not all terrorists are made because of their similar circumstances. That notion doesn't really have research support anymore.

In addition, since 1992, terrorism has been a feature of "Israel's relationship with Palestine" and Soibelman (2004) subscribes to the group processes idea over individual's psychology like personality. Due to the researcher rejects the idea that suicide bombers are simply young religious fanatics and instead believes less extreme personality characteristics make up bombers. This was based on his research and interviews with 5 suicide bombers that were arrested before they could carry out the attack or the bombs failed to detonate (something that happens in another 40% of suicide bombings). The results of his interviews show there wasn't a single explanation for why they became terrorists and instead there was a mixture of factors that were responsible but even this mixture was different for different terrorists.

Yet it seemed that group solidarity and having a shared ideology were two overriding factors in becoming a terrorist because most of the interviewed suicide bombers had at least some shared ideology and solidarity.

Furthermore, political factors were given as reasons for becoming suicide bombers, as well as having bad or secondary experience of dealing with the Israeli defence force. Such as the Israelis shooting one of their friends or beating them.

And this is what I find interesting, most of the suicide bombers had been involved in protests or another form of assembly beforehand they were involved in terrorism. That means these people once wanted change through peaceful means and something changed to make them believe terrorism was the only option.

To explain this, Soibelman (2004) suggested as the situation escalates, a person's beliefs get more extreme. As well as given the nature of the sample, these suicide bombers were a part of the secular Fatah movement, so religion wasn't a factor in them becoming terrorists. And despite this terrorist group don't tend to have criminal histories, a few of them could have.

Another study that offers up a more detailed account of the range of factors impacting someone's chance of becoming a terrorist can be found in Sarangi and Alison's (2005) and their study of the left-wing Maoist terrorists in Nepal and India. This terror group believe the state is an instrument of the rich and needs to be violently overthrown.

The researchers interviewed 12 terrorists and 3 men and 3 women that were no longer involved with their average age being 26 years old and they generally lacked a formal education. These interviews were validated by checking court and police records.

In this study, rapport building was a priority and the researches achieved this by having the terrorists talk about their childhood and matters not directly tied to terrorist activities. Then the researchers suggested common rhetorical structures in the interview.

The results of the interviews showed that the terrorists had created a strong sense of "Us" (which included their Self-Image) and they saw themselves as a central character for themselves in their life story as brave, good, simple, logical and so on. Instead of the reality when the terrorist spoke about themselves, their family, friends and other people in their community being poor simple, naive, exploited, short on goods and water and cheated by others.

Also, the interviews showed interpersonal figures were important and included rhetoric about outgroups and others. For example, one rhetoric found was about their beliefs surrounding the government being characteristic of rich, powerful, villain, uncaring and inhuman.

Overall, this study found that terrorists believe themselves to be heroes and very good people that are fighting against an outgroup that is evil and foul and needs to be defeated. This sense of them being heroes helps them maintain their positive self-image and they see their friends and family and local communities as suffering at the hands of the outgroup. Hence, why the outgroup needs to suffer for this perceived injustice.

In conclusion, if these past two chapters have taught you anything, I think we have to conclude that there really is no single factor that causes someone to become a terrorist. It is a mixture of individual, group and political factors that interact together to help make people into a terrorist.

So now we understand how terrorists are made, how do terrorist ideologies and mental processes supporting these extreme ideologies develop?

TERRORIST IDEAOLOGIES AND COGNITION

At this point in the book, we've looked at an introduction to terrorism, any personality or mental health factors that could cause someone to become a terrorist and all of these explanations have basically failed to explain how a terrorist ideology and cognition develops. Therefore, let's zero in on this research area and ask ourselves this pressing question.

Since I think we can all understand that it must take a very specific set of cognitive factors for someone to develop an ideology and set of mental processes that support bombings, mass terror events and other acts of terrorism, like hostage-taking.

As a result, this area of research focuses on the ideological and cognitive changes that are common to help us understand the terrorist journey. Therefore, Borum (2004) proposes that in order to understand terrorism, it is critical to understand that terrorist ideologies are often favourable towards and justify a particular pattern. As well as these ideologies involve an erosion of normal human inhibitions against killing because of the influence of environmental and social changes in the perception of the situation.

This is a logical argument because the vast majority of us have done social psychology before and we understand the importance of people maintaining a positive self-image, so it makes sense that a person would have to develop cognitive processes justifying and supporting their actions. Otherwise, they would feel bad about themselves and no one wants that for self-image and mental health reasons.

In addition, Brown (2004) argued there are 3 conditions that result in a person developing an ideology supporting terrorism. These conditions are the ideology must be characteristic by rigid orthodoxies that don't allow these beliefs to be challenged or questioned in any way. Also, the terrorist ideology must involve beliefs that both justify and guide the terrorist acts.

This is similar to what we saw earlier in the book about True Believers, suicide bombers and more. They truly believe what they're doing is right and when their leadership asks them to act, they don't question their actions regardless of whoever it kills.

Furthermore, building upon the point I made earlier about how terrorist maintain a positive self-image, Bandura (1990) refers to an techniques of moral disengagement. This is important because this disengagement from morality allows terrorists to insulate themselves from the psychological consequences of their actions.

Some of these moral disengagement strategies include dehumanising the victim and coming up with various moral justifications. For example, their act of terrorism is them fighting some evil or grand injustice. As well as other strategies include, minimizing the suffering of their victims and displacement of responsibility by shifting it from themselves to their leaders or others in group. Therefore, this allows the terrorists to disown their agency in the act.

Finally, Beck (2002) demonstrated how terrorists exhibit thinking that shows cognitive distortions that are similar to the distortions found in non-terrorists that carry out violent acts. For instance, terrorists overgeneralise the enemy's failings to encompass whole populations instead of who's really at fault, their perceptions are very white and black with no grey areas as well as terrorists form tunnel vision by focusing on deconstruction of targets.

On the whole, by the end of this chapter, we can see that there are a number of different cognitive changes that develop within a person that allows them to develop a terrorist ideology and cognition. These cognitive changes include using moral disengagement strategies, cognitive distortions and developing rigid orthodoxies that result in their actions being unquestioned.

As heartbreaking as this all is because of the horrific outcomes terrorism can cause, I think this is really interesting to look at because it allows us to understand that social and environmental causes do have a massive impact on a person's behaviour. But also, if we understand how these cognitive changes happen in the first place then we can hopefully start to apply this research in ways that allow us to target these cognitions in deradicalisation programmes.

So now we understand the cognition of a terrorist, we have to ask ourselves the very interesting question of, how do terrorists plan terror attacks?

HOW DO TERRORISTS PLAN TERROR ATTACKS?

Now as a mystery writer, this topic got me very excited to learn about because there are times when I need to know how terrorists might react and plan out an attack. As well as I generally think that everyone is interested in this topic because it can't be easy planning a terror attack when we consider security, finding a target and getting the resources together in order to carry out the attack.

Therefore, when I found out there was "research" on this topic I was rather excited.

However, yet again, we need to accept that this is a very difficult area to research because it's hard to get viable data, because what terrorist would want to reveal how they planned an attack?

Not many.

As a result, researchers have settled for a much less empirical approach to the topic of planning terror attacks. It is even so bad that there are entire academically published articles that contain no data. Instead they are simply speculative, conjecture or entirely theoretical in nature.

Personally, I don't really blame the researchers because they are trying to research the impossible and this must be difficult. Yet psychology is a science so they should at least attempt to be empirical about it and collect empirically validate data to support and draw conclusions from.

Anyway, as you can tell, there is a desperate need for empirical data on the topic.

Thankfully, there's an approach to research by Romyn and Kebbell (2013) that helps us to fill in this gap to some extent. Since these researchers stimulated the planning of a terrorist attack using non-terrorists. For their study, they had "Red Team" Australians in 2 groups with no anti-terrorism training and then another single group with anti-terrorism training.

Then there was Blue Team who was meant to anticipate how the Red Team would attack as well as this group was made up of people with anti-terrorism training like police officers.

The results of the study showed that all the groups ranked the steps involved in planning an attack as the same regardless of their training, but there were differences in how important each step was. For example, the step of "getting weapons" and "identifying targets" were seen as the most important. Also, there was a lot of consistency in targets chosen by the different groups.

As a result of the most popular targets were:

- Underground railway station
- Football cup final
- Military march
- Airport
- Religious gathering

- Electrical substations
- Military base

In addition, there were a lot of similarities in the ordering of targets between the Red and Blue teams with the main reason for the targets being chosen as the expectation of higher causalities and security. As well as the stages involved in the attack. For example:

- Selection of targets
- Get information from internet
- Select location of attack
- In-person recon of location
- Acquire necessary weapons
- Test the weapons

Personally, I think this is rather useful and interesting because it shows us how normal non-terrorists might go about researching and planning a terror attack. And I suppose the mystery writer in me gets interested in the possible storylines that can come off this study. For example, what would happen if some participants who took part in this research then wanted to make their attack real? That would be a lot of fun to write up actually.

However, I have to admit that this research has very limited usefulness in reality, because it is so artificial. These aren't even terrorists for starters so they would lack the drive, the motivation and to be honest, probably the resources to even pull this off. Then again, that might not be much of a valid criticism because of the new wave of lone wolf terrorists.

As a result, future research would dramatically need to improve the methodology and hopefully future research would include interviews with retired or captured terrorists.

So now we understand how terrorists plan terror attacks, what happens when terrorist organisations collapse?

HOW DO TERRORIST ORGANISATIONS END?

I think the vast majority of the content in this book are topics that we think about once in a while. For example, what do all terrorists have a mental health condition, how do terrorists plan attacks and later on, why do people take hostages? Yet even I have to admit that no one really thinks about terrorist organisations ending, until we're asked too.

I suppose in a way one of the only major terrorist organisations that I know about ending is Islamic State and then now I think about it, I know the Ireland Republican Army ended in the 70s. Yet both of those organisations have morphed and changed and returned as something else, just nothing as powerful as they once were.

Therefore, we need to learn upfront that terrorist organisations do end and this is a very poorly understood area of research. Partly this is because it's relatively new and it's only started to receive research interest recently, but also because you really have to be watching terrorist organisations to realise when they've started, when was their peak year and when they've ended.

One research study looking at this topic is Reinares (2011) who interviewed former members of Euskadi Ta Askatasuma (ETA) who had left the organisation before it closed in the 2000s. The researchers found that the key to the organisation's fall was the death of Spanish Dictator Franco in 1975 as Spain became a democracy and there was political decentralisation.

For the ETA's members these political and social changes were enough. And the Basques people were also changing their attitudes towards separatism and violence. In other words, members believed the terror group had achieved its aims so there was no longer any point in being active members. Whereas other people left for reasons that can only be described as personal.

As well as it's worth noting that the members who left didn't become more militant or deracialised, and some former members still strongly believed in the doctrines of violence they agreed to when they joined. Therefore, we could judge that sometimes terrorists leave organisations not because they don't belief in the "mission" anymore or because they're too militant or disillusioned with the organisation, they could leave for personal or other reasons.

In addition, other former members were expelled by the ETA leadership and there were some findings on the circumstances of the members abandoning membership which was useful as it shed some light on the topic.

Due to some people left the ETA when they were still active members but this was uncommon. Since it was more likely that the terrorists left the organisation to hide out in countries like Latin America and France for long periods of time to avoid being arrested.

Finally, the vast majority of former members decided to quit, often during a very long prison sentence. Or because of the development of new reasons, like becoming a father.

On the whole, I wanted to show you that the research suggests that there is absolutely no one reason explaining why terrorists quit organisations, because there is a lot of internal and external reasons explaining why this happens.

Yet there were patterns and it seems clear that people flat out didn't abandon their terrorist ideology and radicalisation because of guilt. That is almost the only reason we can rule out for why people quit terror organisations.

Moreover, building upon the patterns in the ending of terrorist organisations, Miller (2012) studied the statistical patterns of the onset and decline of terrorist organisations using data from the global terrorism database. This database contains data on over 500 groups active between 1970 and 2008. As well as for the terror groups to be included in the study they had to have been active for at least a year.

Miller found there were two major patterns, which were 80% of terrorist groups had a rapid decline from terrorism activity after their peak year of attack, whereas only 20% had a minimal decline after peak year.

In other words, it was the terrorist organisations that had fast-climbing onset curves for attacks that were the most likely to achieve moderate to high levels of attacks per year. As well as terrorist organisations can show rapid or steady decline after their peak year. So the majority of terror groups fall quickly after their peak year but some groups survive a little longer and manage a slow decline in activity.

Although, as I mentioned earlier and I doubt there is much empirical research on the topic given how new this topic is in the literature, but it's critical to understand that just because one terror group ends. It still may signal the start of a new terrorist organisation, like a splinter terror group. For example, how the New IRA rose from the ashes of the original IRA.

So after being introduced to the forensic psychology of terrorism, what's the research behind hostage taking?

I'm really looking forward to the next section because the research improves and we talk about some utterly fascinating findings. So turn over the page and let's learn about hostage situations.

INTRODUCTION TO HOSTAGE BARRICADE INCIDENTS

Moving onto the last section of the book, I am very excited to look at Hostage Barricade Incidents, which I have to admit is a very technical name for hostage situations. And I'm interested in these types of crimes because they are a great plot device in a lot of TV, movies and books as well as I have been known to use a hostage situation from time to time. For example, in my enthralling, gripping private eye novella *Cops, Robbers and Private Eyes.*

However, let's see how these Hostage Barricade Incidents work in reality and how can we use forensic psychology research to better understand these complex, deadly and distressing situations.

As a result, you can probably imagine, Hostage Barricade Incidents describes when the police and security services besiege a place where people are being held against their will. Also, these situations differ from a "normal" or "simple" siege because these sieges don't involve hostages. In these situations the police are trying to get a person out of a physical location.

Whereas in Hostage Barricade Incidents, it isn't the police that are more likely to determine what action is taken and when like in a siege, instead it is the hostage takers that are more likely to determine the action taken by everyone.

One example of this is that the police cannot simply storm in and try to forcibly release the hostages because this is extremely risky and the hostage takers are probably prepared for this action. And you only need to go online to see the different cases when the police had tried to force the release of hostages and hostages have been killed as a result.

Consequently, in Hostage Barricade Incidents, it is flat out critical that there is some form of assessment that takes place so the police and other professionals can be aware of the risk of a forceful intervention compared to continuing the barricade into the future.

This is important to understand for information I'll share later in the book.

To test this in the real-world, Yokota, Iwami, Watanabe, Fiyita and Watanabe (2004) studied risk factors that they established from real-life hostage incidents and compared them to the beliefs police officers have about different aspects of the incidents.

The results show that in real-life Hostage Barricade Incidents, 50% of them had firearms present. So this was a rather poor indicator of risk because firearm use is very common in Hostage Barricade Incidents.

In addition, the researchers found that hostages were more likely to be injured when they were in a domestic setting and when domestic violence was a motive, or when the purpose of the hostage situation was to get ex-partner back with them.

Personally, I always have find that reason very interesting because in my mind, it just doesn't compute because I don't understand how taking a lot of people hostage is going to make anyone fall in love and want to be with someone. And even if that did work, I think for someone to find that attractive and want to get with someone, then my question is, what the hell is wrong with them and if that's what they find attractive then you probably don't want to be with them.

Anyway, that's just my two cents.

Furthermore, the researchers found that expressive situations like suicide, suicide attempts and domestic violence were all more likely to lead to injury. As well as what I find interesting is that the risk of hostages being injured was actually rather low if the perpetrator had a mental health condition.

In addition, the researchers found that 73% of Japanese Police Officers believed if they were in a highly excited state, this was dangerous for hostage takers. In reality, if we look at real-life incidents, it is the longer sieges that increase the risk of death.

Despite the overall risk of hostage deaths being small because fewer than 4% of Hostage Barricade Incidents result in deaths.

The second most common perceived risk factor was "an accident is caused due to interpersonal problems" because this was mentioned by 24% of police officers and the other risk factors are listed below:

- 16% of police officers said telling hostages their demands couldn't be met was risky.
- 33% of officers mentioned offence characteristics were risky. These offence characteristics include a hostage taker's mental health and if they had ever attempted suicide, and drug use.
- 16% of officers mentioned the police were risk factors. For example, if no effective communication between the police and hostage takers could be established.

The second part of Yokota, Iwami, Watanabe, Fiyita and Watanabe (2004) involved getting the police officers to look at 22 possible Hostage Barricade Incidents and getting them to evaluate the risk involved in each one. The descriptions in each of these scenarios included if the hostages were killed or injured, how long the siege was in duration and if the hostage taker had demanded an escape route. As well as there if there was a plane hijacked and if the hostage takers had done this as part of some political action or group. For example, a right-wing terrorism group.

The results showed that generally all these details and risk factors were rated as high risk. When hostages had been injured this was deemed the most high risk, followed by the hostage takers taking illegal drugs followed by the takers being mentally "ill" (I hate that term but it is what is sadly used in the literature).

In addition, the results showed that the police officers rated some low-risk characteristics too. For example, a hostage situation was deemed low risk when the hostage takers made reasonable demands to the police, like demands for money, and when the hostage situation was covered by the media as was the means of escape.

Furthermore, this I don't find very surprising but it is always good to have beliefs confirmed by research. The study found that the police rated emotional and impulsive situations as riskier than instrumental ones. In other words, the police officers believed it is more dangerous and risky when someone has taken hostages because they're extremely emotional, desperate and they haven't put much thought or planning in this.

However, if you've read my book *Police Psychology* then you'll probably be familiar with how there is a difference (sometimes a massive difference) between the beliefs of police officers and what the research says actually happens. These hostage incidents are no different. Due to the researchers found there was a very weak relationship between what police officers judged as risky situations and the injuries and deaths that occurred.

As a result, one obvious conclusion from the study is that officers were unaware of the nature of risk in these hostage situations. Now, this could be a result of inexperience but the study's sample were the sort of officers who would be in control of early stages of hostage negotiations as well as the barricade, so these are the exact sort of people that need to have good awareness of risk early on.

A piece of evidence possibly supporting the argument that this conclusion is a result of inexperience is that 80% of police officers involved in major incidents have less than 5 years of policing experience.

Building upon this further, this idea of a lack of experience can be showed in a model used for senior UK officers who manage major incidents as described by Crego and Alison (2004). Since police officers perceived themselves as having a lack of control and they believe they're going to get the blame whatever happens here as would their managers, so this doesn't help the situation. This results in the police officers deeming hostage situations as complex and difficult to deal with, this is only increased by feelings of lack of experience.

To further research this, Crego and Alison (2004) used electronic conferencing to bring together a range of officers who had managed major incidents in the past. Then they all systematically explored the experience of each person and how they managed the incident.

The aspects of the situation the study looked at included an unstructured account from each person so they told everyone about their experiences and outlined significant issue with the incidents. Then they were given a building, split into teams and they all reviewed the data from the first stage to build on it and there was a plenary session were themes were developed and agreed by everyone.

The results of this study found that professionals focused on prioritisation during hostage incidents because the participants rated different issues according to different criteria. For example, in order of implementation and the impact it would have on the situation. As well as officers used two co-occurring issues as defining features of criticality of incident.

In addition, two important features named by the participants as having a direct impact on hostage barricade incidents are creating a good team atmosphere and keeping both local as well as national police agencies informed.

Then whether the issue would affect how other people judged the police impacted their response. For example, how victims, the local community and media would judge them. This is why police officers try to engage with the media early on in a situation, they anticipate leaks and they appreciate the media as a source of information for them.

Therefore, now we've been introduced to hostage situations, let's see how hostage negotiations work and why they're so important in these potentially deadly situations.

HOSTAGE NEGOTIATIONS

One of my favourite TV series of all time has to be the brilliant programme called "Ransom" which follows a hostage negotiator as he and his team travel the world trying to resolve hostage situations peacefully and they tend to solve larger crimes along the way. Of course, I know full-well that this programme doesn't reflect real hostage situations perfectly and there are probably a few artistic liberties the writers took, but it feels real. And it definitely got me interested in our current chapter.

As a result, the reason why hostage-taking is a separate section of the book is because whilst hostage taking is a terrorist technique, it is more likely to occur in domestic crimes. Such as, armed robberies. And because these crimes are complex and potentially deadly, the practicalities of how to deal with these situations has been addressed by a lot of people, including psychologists.

Part of the reason why psychologists are interested in hostage-taking is because these extreme situations might have a core of morality and there are a lot of psychological factors and processes happening here. Even more so when we consider the hostage takers-police relationship that occurs in these incidents.

This led to Wilson and Smith (2010) proposing that behaviours in hostage takings are bound by 2 rules sets. Firstly, rules about the "normal" behaviour that should be glowed in these situations (in other words what the hostage takers believe is normal in a hostage situation) and these hostage-taking behaviours are bound by rules about everyday behaviour that act as fallbacks if the specific rules cannot be applied.

Furthermore, Wilson and Smith (2010) propose the following are important to understand in these situations. The motivation for the incident is important and this might be complex to figure out but clues to these motivations could be in the behaviour showed in the situation. Since according to Wilson and Smith if the hostage takers only demand money then the incident is personally motivated, not politically.

Whereas if the demand is for the release of fellow terrorists then the hostage takers could be attempting to fill a gap in the organisation. As well as a demand to release prisoners more generally could simply be about terrorist ideology about the perceived injustice of it all.

Another aspect that is important to understand is the level of planning and resources, because the amount of planning could tell us various things. For example, it could indicate the terrorist's determination to fulfil their mission. Also, the terrorist's behaviour should be predictable compared to random incidents. And in case you're wondering how the police would know the level of planning, one such indicator would be the amount of resources the hostage takers have.

What Are The Rules For Negotiation?

As we continue our look at Wilson and

Smith (2010), the researchers suggested a number of rules that negotiators should use in crisis negotiations. For example, Wilson and Smith (2010) strongly believed both parties (the police and the hostage takers) should show that they are willing to negotiate, as well as both parties can show this willingness by several different actions. Such as being willing to extent deadlines to the other party.

Another rule is that the hostages are the currency of this exchange so the terrorists or hostage takes might bargain and/ or negotiate with them. Yet if the hostage takers release all the hostages then this is a bad strategy as only the building or aircraft or whatever the hostage takers are in remain to be bargained with.

On the other hand, if the hostage takers do not release some of the hostages then this is a bad strategy as well. Since this shows they are unwilling to negotiate and this violates the first rule of negotiation. Also, there are other reasons why hostage takers should release some of the hostages because this can earn them good publicity and even more so if some of the released people are women, children and the sick.

On the whole, Wilson and Smith (2010) suggest that deviating from these rules of negotiation might lead to a direct response from the authorities. They give examples about the terrorists bluffing, for instance, about number or whether they have hostages in the first place, because negotiations tend to break down here if this happens.

Guidelines For Hostage Negotiation

Another study that helps to shred some light on how hostage negotiations work in the real world is Flood (2003) who found that 82% of hostage incidents are dealt with without any death or injuries to hostages or hostage takers. This is probably mainly a result of the modern crisis negotiation techniques introduced by Frank Bolz and Harvey Schlossberg of the New York Police Department in the early 1970s.

Now this is interesting because Schlossberg had a doctorate in clinical psychology (Strentz, 2006), and that's only really interesting to me because that's my background, but it means he was very psychologically and academically minded.

The two researchers worked together after the Munich Olympics Massacre where the police tactic used had been disastrous, so the researchers wanted to produce solid guidelines for negotiators in these situations.

Therefore, instead of the hard-nosed, confrontational tactics of the past, Frank Bolz and Harvey Schlossberg introduced new techniques based on conflict and dispute resolution.

Overall, the fundamental principle of their new approach was to buy more time for the police to find a rational ending to the incident, and this approach is critical because it is the fundamental approach that modern negotiations are based on.

In addition, some other parts of the guidelines include how any negotiation with hostage takers takes place whilst the police are focused on containing them in their environment at the same time as they're trying to meet the demands of the takers.

Also, Frank Bolz and Harvey Schlossberg suggest police officers should use whatever methods are available to them to understand the motives of the hostage takers and personality factors that might underline the incident.

With an extremely important aspect being that the police officers to proceed with the negotiations at a purposefully slow pace to stretch out the time for negotiating. This is a possible way of dealing with the already stretched emotion of the hostage takers by giving them more time to express how they feel and so on might react in a more rational way.

The Sheer Importance Of Active Listening Skills In Hostage Negotiations

To wrap up this chapter on hostage negotiations before we move onto the various models, we need to talk about "Active listening skills" because this is a phrase used to describe strategies like mirroring and emotional labelling that is involving in the formation of a relationship between the hostage takers and the negotiators. Hopefully, leading to a diffusion of the situation.

Noesner and Webster (1997) describes different types of active listening skills used in these types of the situation. For example, paraphrasing, this is where the hostage takers' words are repeated back by the negotiator in their own words to show the hostage takers they're being listened too. Also, open ended questions are a good example because these are the only way to learn what's going on. Since when the hostage takers do most of the talking, it means they're giving longer responses and they can reveal more information to the negotiators.

In addition, another example of active listening is minimal encouragement. This is where the negotiators show the hostage takers they're listening by keeping the conversation going and this can result in control of the situation shifting to the negotiator. Everyday examples of these "encouragements" include "okay" and "I see".

Also, you can have emotional labelling where the negotiator needs to deal with the hostage taker's emotion about the incident. So the negotiator gives the hostage taker's emotion a tentative label. For example, "you seen to be angry with how the English have treated Muslims in their country," then the taker's response to the statement allows the negotiator to learn more.

Furthermore, mirroring involves repeating a few words of what the hostage taker just said. Such as if the taker said "I won't let some English push me around," the negotiator might say "You won't let the English push you around,". This is effective because it avoids a confrontational stance between the takers and the police and it might reveal more information.

Finally, "I" messages can be useful because these are non-confrontational personal comments that the negotiator makes in response in the hostage taker's words actions. For example, them talking about their own frustration about lack of professional negotiators.

Thankfully, a person doesn't have to be a born negotiator to be good at it, because hostage negotiation can be a taught skill in police training programmes.

Due to Perera et al. (2006) evaluated a training programme with psychological, suicide prevention, basic negotiation principles and more taught through role play. Then FBI agents took part in the role play assessment before and after the intensive training. As well as the role-play for the negotiation skills were based on real-life audio tapes from incidents.

The results showed that the agents' active listening generally improved after the training.

Nonetheless, one interesting finding from the study was that problem solving decreased after training. And it is suggested that this might be a good thing because it is dangerous if the police officers try to come on with a solution before any rapport has been developed between the police and the hostage takers. Therefore, if problem solving happens in the early stages of incidents then this could very well increase the likelihood of a pre-emptive intervention so this is dangerous for everyone involved.

On the whole, it's clear that hostage negotiation skills can be taught, but there is evidence that these active listening skills aren't used in practice.

This mainly comes from Webster (2004) who listened to audiotapes from real life incidents and the study found that only 13% used active listening skills. And out of 13%, 66% of these skills were minor encouragements. Such as very basic acknowledgements that the negotiators was listening. Like repeating what was said.

Also, complex active listening skills were a much smaller total of the 13%. For example, 66% might have been minor encouragement but 12% was paraphrasing, 8% of total was emotional labelling, 7% of total was summarising and 6% of the officer's turn to speak was mirroring. If minor encouragements were taken out only 6% of the total are active listening skills. That's a decrease of 7%.

Overall, whilst research shows that active listening skills are flat out critical in real-world hostage negotiations, it is a shame and clear that these skills are not being used in practice.

So now we've been introduced to hostage negotiations and the different skills and concepts and rules needed for them, I wonder are there any psychological models that bring all this knowledge together?

MODELS OF HOSTAGE NEGOTIATION

As most of the readers of this book are going to be university psychology students or psychology professionals, I think it is safe to say that we are all aware of psychology's love of models. Us psychologists flat out love a good model to help explain stuff, how different processes work and models seem to be the cool thing to do in psychology.

Of course, I am well aware that psychological models are really important and they are very useful in helping us conceptualise and understand different psychological processes.

However, when it comes to hostage negotiations these models can be a little… silly to some extent. Since there are so many different models and most of them are just theoretical with only a handful of them actually being evidence-based.

Some reason or piece of supporting evidence for why the empirical research literature on terrorism is so dire and just awful.

Then again, I need to remind all of us, including myself, that most of the time psychologists do adopt the empirical models but as we know from previous chapters, conducting empirical work on terrorism is very difficult or next to impossible.

Overall, the entire purpose of a psychological model is to offer researchers a way to clarify a very difficult and complex problem into something that is easier to understand. Of course, there are massive problems with this approach because we are probably trying to "dumb down" massive psychological concepts into a nice, tidy little model. Yet that argument is outside the scope of this book.

In addition, this lack of evidence-based models needs to be addressed urgently because crisis negotiations are deadly issues were people could die if a mistake is made, so it is critical that we understand how these negotiations work. Both in a theoretical sense and in a real-world sense.

In addition, different models provide police officers with a shared framework and a basis for going forward with any crisis negotiations. With the wonderfully added caveat (that protects the authors of models from blame) that all models need to be used flexibly and police officers might need to move back a stage as the negotiations go forward.

FBI's Behavioural Influence Stairway Model of Crisis Negotiation

This model of crisis negotiation was created by Vecchi, Van Hasselt and Romano (2005) and according to Ireland and Vecchi (2009), this was a protype version of this sort of model that went onto influenced strategies in UK.

Therefore, FBI's Behavioural Influence Stairway Model of Crisis Negotiation is the updated version of the original FBI model. As well as the stairway metaphor is common in crisis negotiation models, because the stairway starts at the bottom where there is no relationship between the negotiators and hostage takers. Then it ends at the top of the stairs where there is a good relationship between the hostage takers and negotiators.

When it comes to how the negotiators get from the bottom step to the top step, the progress is done by active listening skills over time and a few other factors that we'll look at in this chapter. Yet these steps are flexible to circumstances because sometimes negotiators just don't have time to build a relationship like they normally would.

Moreover, there is no reason for negotiators to take a step down in face of difficulty. As well as there's no fixed time scale, negotiators don't need to know anything about if the hostage takers have any mental health conditions and negotiators don't really need to know their motives for this model.

What Is The Process Of Bringing The Incident To Peaceful Resolution?

We all probably know by now that the underlying aim of hostage negotiation is to build a relationship between the police and the hostage takers by developing trust and positive relationships. The aim of hostage negotiations are not to understand the motives of the hostage taker.

The reason for this is because if you concentrate on the motives then this causes a divergence away from the emotionally driven aspects of the situation and can make matters worse.

Also, it's important to note that hostage negotiators are not there to solve the problems of the terrorists.

I'm mentioning all of this because building a relationship in "normal" circumstances requires a lot of give and take, a lot of time and a lot of effort from both parties. You don't have this time and other luxuries in a hostage situation, so there is a stairway dynamic and terrorists might alternate between different steps of these models.

Then if we cast our minds back to the last chapter, active listening skills can be critical and they can thought of as moving a terrorist from a place of emotionally to rationality, so you can talk them down and end the situation peacefully.

As a result, the stages used in this FBI model are empathy, rapport and influence. Yet thankfully, there is a lot of flexibility in the model and this is important because as I just mentioned, relationships go back and forth on the steps. But the model is still useful as it brings a sense of structure to a situation that is often chaotic to the negotiator involved.

Moreover, Madrignal, Bowman and McClain (2009) suggested a 4 phase model that focuses on the action of the negotiator and indicates what style of negotiation to take. These phases are establishing the initial dialogue, building rapport, influencing and surrender. As well as all these phases require different types of verbal statements so they change throughout the process and backtracking is possible to. Also, it's important that this process isn't done too quickly as this could result in the hostage takers becoming angry or have some sort of other reaction.

And talking more generally for a moment, phase 1 needs to be done correctly to stop the taker's response becoming very negative in phase 2. Hence, why active listening skills are critical.

When it comes to establishing the initial dialogue, the police are assuming that the hostage taker could be reluctant to talk to a negotiator and maybe hostile. So this stage is about creating a dialogue by whatever means are appropriate. Once a dialogue is created, the initial statements used by the negotiators are more general and about the situation compared to later stages. Some topics can actually include the weather and talking about the condition of the hostages and even a sports game if the hostage situation is happening on a day of a big match. Although, this phase is difficult because the hostage taker might not want to talk to the police or any negotiator.

In terms of building rapport, the purpose of this stage is to create a personal relationship between the hostage taker and the negotiator where the free exchange of personal information becomes available.

Also, a negotiator can know if they've been successful in this stage because the hostage taker will be able to tell them information including things about their emotions.

Penultimately, there is the influencing with the task of this stage meaning the negotiator needs to persuade the hostage takers to free the hostages and bring the stand-off to a peaceful end. The risk at this stage is if the hostage taker believes the negotiator is trying to trick them into something then this can get risky very quickly. Thankfully, because there is already a personal relationship between the taker and the negotiator, there aren't many active listening skills needed here so the negotiator might be able to make suggestions, promises and try to reframe the situation as a positive outcome for surrender.

And even the negotiator providing solutions to the problem and bargaining could be a part of this phase, this isn't the focus. The focus will always be communicating to the hostage taker about the safety of surrender peacefully.

Finally, surrender is obviously when the hostage taker has decided to surrender. Then it becomes the job of the negotiator to give the hostage takers instructions about how to do it safely and ensure takers know what is required.

I do personally quite like this model because it seems good, useful and rather practical which in these sort of situations is always good.

On the whole, the model might not be built on vast amounts of research but it is extremely useful in conceptualising and breaking down the negotiation process so negotiators can structure their experiences around a meaningful framework.

Therefore, in this book, so far we've looked at terrorism and hostage taking as two rather separate things, what happens when we combine them? What does the research say about terrorists that take hostages?

HOW TERRORISM LINKS TO HOSTAGE-TAKING?

For the final chapter of the book, we are going to be bringing everything together, because I suppose some of you might have been wondering why we were looking at terrorism and hostage taking situations as very different things. The reason for that is because generally speaking, they are really easy to treat as separate things but sometimes hostage takings are linked to terrorism.

As a result, whilst most hostage takings aren't linked to terrorism, this does happen but this is problematic for the research literature because it strains our current research. Which to be honest by this point in the book, I think it is fair to say that it doesn't exactly take much to strain our current research. And yes I know I don't have a very high opinion of this current literature but considering how artificial and how unempirical it is, I don't really think you can blame me.

Anyway, a brilliant research example but a terrible event in human history of when an act of terrorism involves a hostage situation is the Belsan school attack that left over 300 adults and children dead in 2004. This incident involved 1200 hostages with many of them being children and they were taken by 50 strategically placed hostage takers.

This was made even worse by the fact that 21 people were killed on the first day of the attack and the bodies were thrown out of windows for everyone outside to see.

Also, the terrorists were very clever because they not only had 4 terrorists in a single area, but any 1 of these 4 terrorists in that single area could explode all 130 explosives in other parts of the school.

In addition, the terrorists made impossible demands and this is where you know they were well-prepared. The terrorists made use of gasmasks so that eliminated a wide range of options for the police, and there were angry parents outside the school threatening to kill the rescuers if they didn't try to intervene.

As you can imagine the situation was always only going to have one single outcome. There would be a lot of deaths and I think this is a fascinating example because this was a very well thoughtful terror attack, and if one of my books ever needed an extremely thoughtful hostage situation, I would probably draw on this awful incident for inspiration.

As a result of this incident and others, Dolnick and Fitzgerald (2011) painted a picture of "new terrorists" and this is for a few reasons. Yet new terrorists are difficult to read because they typically study and read hostage taking incident reports and they read hostage crisis training manuals. As well as this new breed of terrorists seem more willing to harm hostages to achieve their aims.

In addition, this new breed seems to have good tactical knowledge so it's difficult to use threats coercively and to bargain hard, because these groups have good weapons and they are prepared to die. As well as they have good communication with fellow terrorists at different locations, and this links back to what I spoke about at the beginning of the book about new waves of terrorism follow advancements in technology.

A final reason or concern surrounding this new breed of terrorists comes from their use of religious rhetoric because there has always been religious rhetoric in terrorism, but the rhetoric used by this new breed of terrorist is extreme and goes far beyond what negotiators have experienced in general.

Therefore, there needs to be resources available to help negotiations as suggested by Dolnick and Fitzgerald.

Since negotiations are about influencing the thinking, decision-making and the behaviour of another person, and just talking with a terrorist or hostage taker can help to provide the negotiators with important information.

When it comes to dealing with terrorists, negotiators need to remember that they're negotiating with a rational person, regardless of the extremeness of their actions. And this I think is always important to bear in mind, in everyday life (let alone dealing with terrorists) there are countless examples of actions we don't personally understand but these actions are perfectly logical to that individual. For example, if we quickly think about depression, to you and me, it makes no sense not doing activities we enjoy to improve our mood, but to a depressed person it is perfectly logical not to do that because they are simply too hard to do and they'll fail at it and all the other negative cognitive processes.

My point is if negotiators start thinking of them as terrorists then this can conjure up stereotypes of terrorism and this might very well be counterproductive. Especially, when we consider that in mainstream society, terrorists are thought to be dumb, irrational, crazy zealots that wouldn't know sense if it bit them in the private area. The reality is very different, something I hope I've showed you in this book.

Therefore, negotiators need to constantly question their assumptions, biases and their characteristics of the terrorists to make sure that they aren't falling into its biased cognitive processes. For example, if the negotiators jump to conclusions then this could result in them missing opportunities for more information that is correct compared to the assumptions the negotiators are making up as well.

Another guideline for negotiation is negotiators should look for a way to empathically address any grievances underlying the hostage taking and terrorist action, because this can make it more difficult for the terrorists to label the authorities negatively as being unreasonable.

In addition, active listening skills should

always be used to get as full a picture as possible about terrorist's motives and grievances, so asking in detail for a justification of the action could be good here.

Overall, there isn't a great amount of research when it comes to terrorism and hostage-taking, let alone when you combine the two areas. Therefore, whilst this is an extremely important research area, it is advancing very slowly on a rather insecurely based that absolutely has to be improved over time.

CONCLUSION

I have to admit that I have really enjoyed this book because it's fun to look at terrorism and hostage-taking from a forensic psychology viewpoint. Since forensic psychology allows us to explore criminal behaviour in an empirical manner and it allows us to overcome the myths and misconceptions that society creates to help itself understand awful actions. This is what we saw in the second chapter when we found that despite popular belief, terrorism is not caused by personality factors or mental health conditions.

In addition, I really enjoyed learning about what actually makes a terrorist, because we might not have all the answers. In fact, we certainly do not have most of the answers, but we are slowly starting to understand stuff and we have finally recognised that it is a wide range of factors that start and maintain someone going on the long road to becoming a terrorist.

Personally, I actually believe this is a good thing. I think it's good that it's a long road and it is a process. It means that there is time, there are opportunities and there is hope of "saving" that person before they become an active terrorist that attacks and kills people.

That is why looking at terrorism and hostage-taking is so important because it is all about hope. Giving us a sense of hope that we can understand this awful behaviour and we can create interventions and support the people that are more likely to become terrorists.

Of course, there are massive research problems and I will never excuse some of the poor research practices. I get researching terrorism is an impossible task but at least these researchers are trying. They might not always succeed and they certainly need to improve their practices to improve their research, but I do appreciate them trying.

All research areas have to start somewhere and I think if we look at all research areas in all sciences, there were questionable things going on in the early days for all of them. But research into terrorism must improve if it is ever going to have the power that it needs, if this research is ever going to have a meaningful impact in society against terrorism.

Therefore, I truly hope that you've learnt a lot from this book and that you're enjoyed it. I know that I have and I look forward to exploring forensic psychology even more in the coming years because forensic psychology is a lot of fun.

Because who doesn't love exploring the darker side of human behaviour. I know I do and I'm willing to say if you're made it to the end of this book, then you probably do to.

REFERENCES

Abbasi, I., Khatwani, M. K., & Soomro, H. A. (2018). A review of psycho-social theories of terrorism. *Grassroots*, *51*(2).

Borum, R. (2004). Psychology of terrorism.

Braithwaite, A. (2013). The logic of public fear in terrorism and counter-terrorism. *Journal of police and criminal psychology*, *28*, 95-101.

DiMaggio, C., & Galea, S. (2006). The behavioral consequences of terrorism: a meta-analysis. *Academic emergency medicine*, *13*(5), 559-566.

DiMaggio, C., Galea, S., & Richardson, L. D. (2007). Emergency department visits for behavioral and mental health care after a terrorist attack. *Annals of Emergency Medicine*, *50*(3), 327-334.

Ferguson, N., & Kamble, S. V. (2012). The role of revenge, denial, and terrorism distress in restoring just world beliefs: the impact of the 2008 Mumbai attacks on British and Indian students. *The Journal of social psychology*, *152*(6), 687-696.

Foster, D. M., Braithwaite, A., & Sobek, D. (2013). There can be no compromise: Institutional inclusiveness, fractionalization and domestic terrorism. *British Journal of Political Science*, *43*(3), 541-557.

Fujita, G., Watanabe, K., Yokota, K., Kuraishi, H., Suzuki, M., Wachi, T., & Otsuka, Y. (2013). Multivariate models for behavioral offender profiling of Japanese homicide. *Criminal Justice and Behavior*, *40*(2), 214-227.

Gabriel, R., Ferrando, L., Cortón, E. S., Mingote, C., García-Camba, E., Liria, A. F., & Galea, S. (2007). Psychopathological consequences after a terrorist attack: An epidemiological study among victims, the general population, and police officers☆. *European Psychiatry*, *22*(6), 339-346.

Howitt, D. (2015). *Introduction to forensic and criminal psychology*. Pearson Education.

Hudson, R. A. (2007). The sociology and psychology of terrorism: Who becomes a terrorist and why?.

Jhangiani, R. (2010). Psychological concomitants of the 11 September 2001 terrorist attacks: A review. *Behavioral Sciences of Terrorism and Political Aggression*, *2*(1), 38-69.

Lipkus, I. (1991). The construction and preliminary validation of a global belief in a just world scale and the exploratory analysis of the multidimensional belief in a just world scale. *Personality and Individual differences*, *12*(11), 1171-1178.

Lomborg, B., & Sandler, T. (2008). Re-thinking counter-terrorism. *Daily News Egypt.*

Mythen, G., & Walklate, S. (2006). Criminology and terrorism: Which thesis? Risk society or governmentality?. *British journal of criminology*, *46*(3), 379-398.

Post, J. M., McGinnis, C., & Moody, K. (2014). The changing face of terrorism in the 21st century: The communications revolution and the virtual community of hatred. *Behavioral sciences & the law*, *32*(3), 306-334.

Silker, E. S. (2004). Terrorists, interrogation, and torture: Where do we draw the line. *J. Legis.*, *31*, 191.

Yokota, K., Fujita, G., Watanabe, K., Yoshimoto, K., & Wachi, T. (2007). Application of the behavioral investigative support system for profiling perpetrators of serial sexual assaults. *Behavioral Sciences & the Law*, *25*(6), 841-856.

AVAILABLE AT ALL MAJOR BOOKSELLERS!

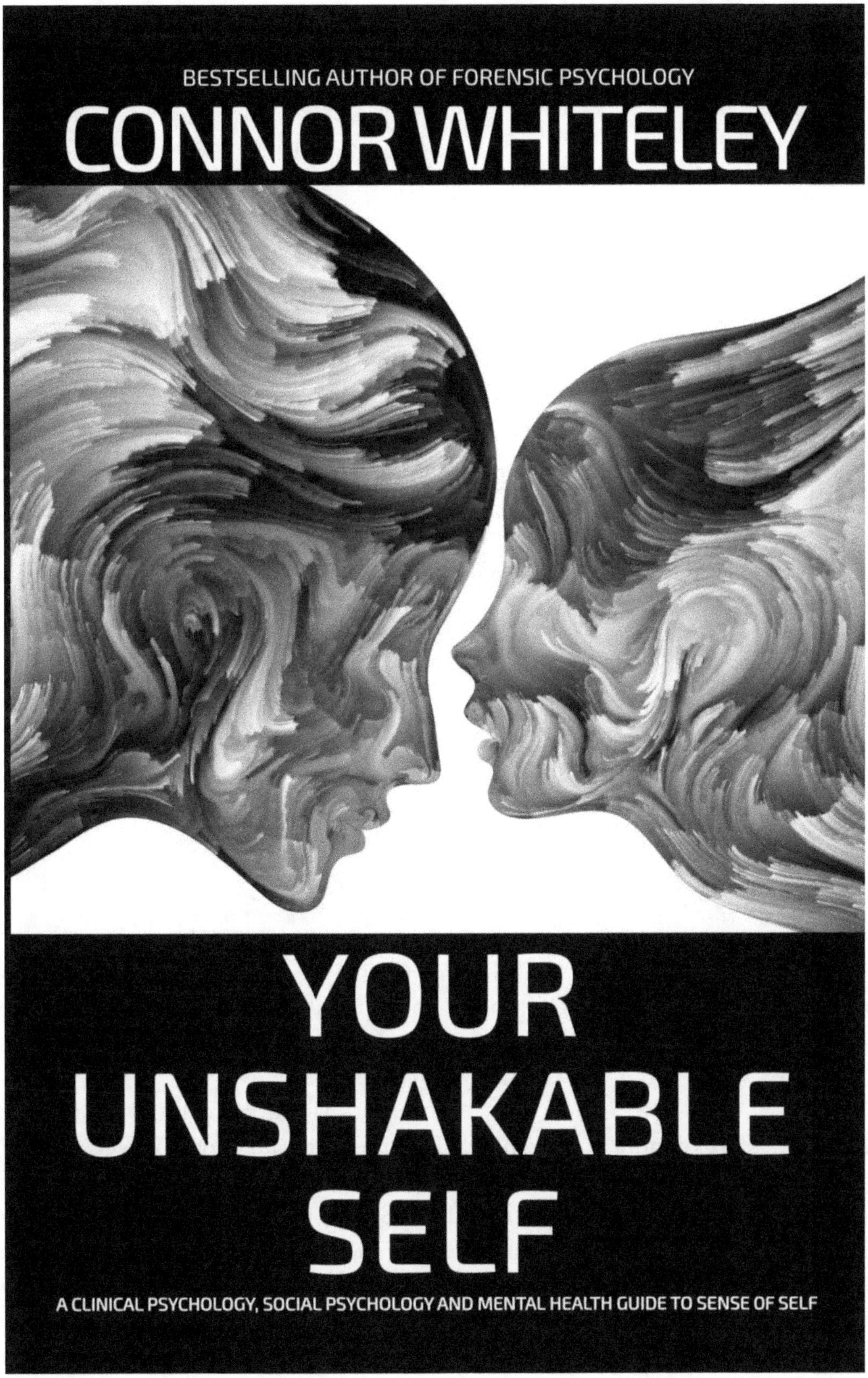
BESTSELLING AUTHOR OF FORENSIC PSYCHOLOGY
CONNOR WHITELEY
YOUR
UNSHAKABLE
SELF
A CLINICAL PSYCHOLOGY, SOCIAL PSYCHOLOGY AND MENTAL HEALTH GUIDE TO SENSE OF SELF

YOUR UNSHAKABLE SELF

A Clinical psychology, Social Psychology and Mental Health Guide to Sense of Self

INTRODUCTION

"As long as I have my unshakable self, I can dig in with both feet with all my might. As long as I know who I am, all my doubts, hesitations, and frustrations will disappear. And no demon on earth can escape my descending blade,"

-Muichiro Tokito, Demonslayer Season 4.

Even if you don't have anorexia, I'll explain why this is a brilliant quote for everyone in a moment.

It is very rare that I find a quote that moves me as much as this one did, and a quote that I believe so accurately depicts mental health challenges at times. Since whether you're a new or long-time reader or listener of The Psychology World Podcast, then you might be aware that I have suffered childhood abuse, rape and anorexia in my life. There were a lot of factors that led to my anorexia, but I think one of the main factors was I was healing from my rape and I simply didn't know who I was without my rape trauma.

Anorexia seemed to be a "good" choice to replace it with.

However, as part of anorexia recovery, you do a lot of exercises to help you realise and think about who you are without the anorexia. You focus on the parts of you that the anorexia has suppressed and as part of recovery, you help those non-anorexia aspects of you shine through.

This is why knowing who you are and building your Unshakable Self has so many mental health benefits. As well as remembering this quote and how I want to build my Unshakable Self so I could get rid of my doubts, my hesitations and my frustrations were a powerful force that helped me in my anorexia recovery.

In addition, I think the part *"And no demon on earth can escape my descending blade,"* doesn't only have to apply in the fantasy context. I think the descending blade can be your empowered self, your strength and your ability to do whatever you put your mind to, and the demon is any challenge that the world throws at you.

Ultimately, this quote is all about saying if you know who you are including your core values, your beliefs and your identity. Then you are able to deal with any challenge the world throws at you.

I completely agree.

What Will This Book Cover?

This book covers a lot of easy-to-understand, engaging and fascinating topics from psychology and mental health to help you understand how to find out who you are, and help you start building your Unshakable Self. Also, the end of each chapter includes several questions to help you reflect on what you learnt in the chapter. As well as I draw on my own mental health experience to bring the material alive.

Some of the topics covered include:

- What Are the Mental Health Benefits of Knowing Who You Are?
- What Is Identity?
- Why Is Our Self-Image So Important?
- What Is Self-Worth and How to Improve It?
- And so much more.

Who Is This Book For?

Normally, my books are written for psychology students and psychology professionals, but this easy-to-understand, fascinating and engaging book is written for anyone who wants to know more about the Self. As well as how to find who they are, improve their mental health and more.

You don't need any psychology knowledge before reading this book and I had a lot of fun researching and writing this book, so I know you're going to enjoy it too.

Who Am I?

Personally, I always love to know who the author is of the nonfiction I read so I know the information is coming from a good source. In case you're like me, I'm Connor Whiteley GMBPsS, the internationally bestselling author of over 50 psychology books.

In addition, I am the host of *The Psychology World Podcast,* a weekly show exploring a new psychology topic each week and delivering the latest psychology news. Available on all major podcast apps and YouTube.

Finally, I am a psychology graduate studying a Clinical Psychology Masters at the

University of Kent, England until September 2025.

So now we know more about each other, let's start exploring the great topic of Your Unshakable Self.

WHAT ARE THE MENTAL HEALTH BENEFITS OF KNOWING YOUR SELF AND VALUES?

A lot of people when it comes to writing believe that nonfiction writers like to hold the "secret" or entire point of the book until the end, but I'm not going to do that. Instead, in this first chapter, I'm going to explain the importance of knowing who you are and what your values are to your mental health immediately.

Afterwards, we'll start to explore the different nuances of the Self and our sense of self can change and become better defined over time. For example, we'll explore the impact of trauma recovery on the Self because this is a major focus of this book too, based on my own experience.

I've only really learnt who I am, how strong I am and exactly what I am capable of surviving because I've healed from several types of trauma throughout my life.

Why Is It Important to Know Who You Are?

Similar to Tokito's quote, once you understand who you are, you're better able to get rid of your doubts and hesitations because you know what guides you in life. If you make decisions in line with your values and your principles then you won't be second-guessing yourself because whatever your decision or choice that you make, you'll know that it was the best possible decision for you at that moment in time.

I'll introduce you to an exercise later on in the first chapter to help you realise what your values are.

For example, I work part-time as a student ambassador for my university in disadvantaged areas, so we can show students that university is an accessible option for them if they desire it. Most of us come from disadvantaged backgrounds ourselves, and this is actually an activity we do with Year 12 (17- and 18-year-olds) to help them make choices about their life that are right for *them*. Not their social group.

For instance, if a year 12 student placed a high value on creativity then they would be happier with their decisions in life if it allowed them to be more creative. Therefore, it might be a good idea for them to choose creative subjects and work towards a creative career instead of, let's say, accounting.

Anyway, knowing who *you* are instead of what other people tell you or your abused or traumatised self is important for mental health too. There will be a lot of different examples and research studies shown throughout the book as we dive into different areas.

Nonetheless, knowing who you are and your values can be immensely valuable and I'm going to use anorexia as an example. You might think anorexia is an extreme example because it is the deadliest mental health condition we know of but anorexia is a clear example of the importance of knowing yourself from a mental health perspective.

And this all generalises to other mental health conditions too and everyday life.

How Knowing Who You Are Helps Anorexia Recovery?

When it comes to anorexia, and this applies to trauma and other mental health conditions as well, a major focus of recovery is amplifying the non-anorexic parts of yourself and pushing the anorexic parts of the Self to one side.

Due to for people with anorexia, like myself, we are often controlled and we often give in to the demands of the anorexia. For example, avoid this food, do not eat that, restrict your intake to this amount and so on. Very quickly the anorexic parts of the Self can grow and this can push away or shrink the other parts of the Self.

As a result, some people suggest that leaving anorexia behind is actually very difficult because they don't know who they are without it. And personally, I think this is why my anorexia got bad in the first place, because whilst I am embarrassed to actually write it down for the first time. I was healing from my rape, childhood trauma and everything in my life was going so well, I felt strange.

I actually write about it in my book *Healing As A Survivor*, it was a very disorientating feeling to actually have great mental health for the first time in my life.

Honestly, I think I might have allowed my anorexia to get clinically significant (to be non-judgmental to myself) so I could stick to what I knew of my Self and what everyone else knew I was like.

This is what a lot of people with anorexia mention because they explain they can feel weird and unsteady as they step away from their anorexia.

However, everyone including myself who falls into this mental trap forgets a critical factor. You will hopefully be able to walk away from your anorexia, and if you've been abused (which anorexia is like an abusive partner) then your abuser might have taken your self-esteem, your-self-confidence and they might have filled you with thousands of doubts and hesitations. Yet there is one thing no one, absolutely no one can ever take from you.

Your core values.

As you start thinking about walking away from your anorexia, and you start thinking about the person you want to be and the life you want to create for yourself, it is important to map out as well as consider your core values. Since you can always take these core values with you and even if your anorexia overshadows them again, your core values will never leave you.

They really won't.

And you can use these core values to craft a life and your new Self beyond your mental health condition and anorexia.

<u>How Do You Know Your Core Values?</u>

There are two ways you can get your list of core values. I'll briefly mention two ways before explaining more about the exercise. Firstly, you can go online and literally type in *list of core values*. I found tons of options including a list of 50 core values and you look through them.

Secondly, you can do what my counsellor got me to do in our third session. You can simply write down your core values.

Examples of core values include:

- Authenticity
- Adventure
- Authority
- Balance
- Compassion

- Challenge
- Community
- Fairness
- Fun
- Growth
- Happiness
- Justice
- Love
- Loyalty
- Openness
- Respect
- Security
- Service
- Trustworthiness
- Wealth
- Wisdom

There are a lot more core values that people can have but you get the general idea.

Afterward, you need to pick *your* top 5 core values. These are the core values that represent *you* the most and they are **most** important to *you.* Then do the same for the 5 **least** important.

For example, my top 5 core values are:

- Creativity
- Curiosity
- Independence
- Lifelong learning
- Supportive

My least important core values are:

- God's will
- Spirituality
- Simplicity
- Fame
- Sexuality

I got these core values from an online table.

Next rank the most important core values in order. For me, it would be:

- Creativity
- Curiosity
- Supportive
- Lifelong learning
- Independence

It is a hard exercise but useful.

After you've done this exercise, you can think about the following:

- Which of my values are most linked with my anorexia side?
- Which values are most linked with my non-anorexic side?
- Have any of your values been exaggerated, sidelined or ignored by anorexia?
- Does your anorexia interfere with your values in any other ways?
- Can your values help you to fight your anorexia?

Personally, I was very surprised at the power of this set of exercises because once you understand your core values and what you hold dearest to you, and you start to understand how anorexia or another mental health condition threatens that. Then that is powerful motivation to change and start recovering.

To go back to Tokito's quote, once I understood that my anorexia was making me so sick that my ability to be creative, curious and learn was threatened. Then all my hesitations and doubts about recovering from my anorexia went away, because if I didn't try and recover from my anorexia then I would not be happy and I would not be in control of my life.

That is something I cannot allow to happen.

Ultimately, at the end of this chapter, I want to stress here that knowing your Self and your core values is immensely important to your mental health. It can give you the strength to make decisions and it can give you the motivation and support and guidance to start the scary journey towards recovering from your mental health condition. Be it depression, trauma or anorexia.

Knowing who you are and what values make you up is so important, and when it comes to a condition as deadly as anorexia. It really can save your life.

WHAT IS IDENTITY?

As we start to explore more of the psychological basis of your Self and your identity, I want to start off with the basics in terms of what actually is our identity. In the next chapter, you'll start learning about the identity theories that social psychologists have come up with over the years. Since whilst a lot of psychology students and professionals have heard of Social Identity Theory amongst other theories to explain the formation of our social identities, what an identity actually is isn't as well understood. Let alone how to live authentically. Our identities are made up of our experiences, our memories, our likes, dislikes and so much more. Therefore, in this chapter, you'll learn what is identity, what is an identity crisis, how to live authentically and more.

What Is Identity?

Our identity is made up of our values, memories, experiences as well as relationships that make up our sense of self. It is this mixture that creates a steady sense of who we are over time and this remains steady even as new facets of our identity are created.

This is important to think about because everyone struggles with basic life questions. For instance, "Who am I?" and "Who do I want to be in the future?" The reason why these questions are so complex is because our identities are complex since our identities are made up of so many different aspects of our Selves. Our identities are made up of our relationships to other people, like us being someone's child, friend, partner and/ or parent. Also, our identity is made up of external characteristics that we don't control, like our socioeconomic status. As well as our identities are made up of our political opinions, religious beliefs and moral attitudes.

All these different factors influence our choices on a daily basis.

Moreover, all of our identities hold multiple roles and each of these roles hold different meanings and expectations that we internalise into our identity. For example, I am a writer, author, podcaster, psychology student, British citizen and so on. My writer Self means I am expected to be creative, entertaining and read a lot (I am all those three things and more) and my student Self means I am expected to be studious, hardworking and clever. So I need to incorporate all those expectations into my identity as well. The same goes for if you're a teacher, a French citizen and a political activist. Each role means something different for you and your identity so you need to incorporate all of these elements into your identity.

In addition, some people will struggle more with their identities than others. For example, people who are very concerned with what other people think of them, or if people have to suppress an important part of themselves, like their gender or sexuality. Equally, if someone reflects on the discrepancy between who they are and who they want to be then this can be a powerful force for change.

Personally, I completely agree because it was one of the reasons why I had a mental breakdown in August 2023 after a decade of intensely homophobic abuse. I didn't want to be the person I was anymore. I wanted to be free, I wanted to live authentically and I didn't want to be in fear for my life anymore, so I made the change and as terrifying as it was, I am really happy that I made the change.

Finally, our identity can influence our relationships because the different facets of our identities can be similar or different to people. For example, similarities between identities could include similar gender, profession, racial background amongst others. In turn, this can help to bring us together or push others away. Then as we know from other areas of social psychology, people form social ingroups based on their shared identity so these people can have stronger senses of kinships with each other.

Why Do People Feel Like They Do Not Understand Themselves?

People largely don't feel like they understand themselves because whilst we all have the goal of nurturing our values as well as making choices that are consistent with our true selves. There will always be some values from our culture or family that we've internalised despite these values not being consistent with our Selves. This causes conflict within ourselves and this drives uncertainty and dissatisfaction.

Again, if you spend the time to reflect on our values then this can bring about change so you could potentially live a more fulfilling life.

What Is an Identity Crisis?

The term *identity crisis* was termed by Erik Erikson, the creator of an eight-stage model to explain identity development, and in his model, he included stages of identity crisis. Then other people later expanded this concept later on. Whilst identity crisis isn't a clinical term, it refers to when someone is experiencing a challenge to their sense of self and it centres round an aspect of their identity. For example, their religion, career choice, gender role or politics.

How Can People Live Authentically?

There is a lot of focus on living authentically and I've spoken about it a few times on the podcast, because living authentically drives our explorations of play, relationships, friendships, fashion, jobs and so much more. This is why when we're in adolescence and young adulthood, we try different styles, friends, activities and more to see what works and what seriously does not for us. We want to find out what is authentically us so regardless of our age and stage of our life, we can be our true selves.

This is important to do because a lot of mid-lifers report whilst they deepen their commitments to their career, their faith, community and family because this matches their self-image. They can also feel very trapped if they don't feel like they created this life for themselves, because they made these life decisions based on values that were not their own. As well as older adults can see their life choices with satisfaction or regret depending on how these life choices were made. If the life choice was based on a value that was true to their Self then they are happier with it.

Furthermore, authenticity is flat out critical when it comes to mental health because there is a correlation between authenticity and a lot of different aspects of mental health. For example, self-esteem, vitality and coping skills. Therefore, if you act in accordance with your core self (also known as self-determination) then you could protect your mental health against a lot of negative mental health outcomes. Also, some experts believe self-determination is one of the three basic psychological needs alongside a sense of relatedness and competence.

Interestingly, some people question how they can live authentically in a world where "fitting in" is important. To answer this people have said that whilst there will always be tension between being yourself and you fitting in with the social group, be it friends or in a career. You should never be completely forthright or deceitful instead you should use the idea that you need to achieve a balance. This balance is between as long as you are not being forced to act in a way that is the opposite of your values or personality, but you need to self-monitor in case you're then a little self-monitoring will be good.

Another question regarding authenticity is whether people actually can live authentically within relationships. The answer is yes you can, because our relationships become threatened when there is a disconnect between freely expressing yourself and taking your partner's feelings into account. There is the *Authenticity In Relationships Scale* that you can use to see if you need to have conversations about authenticity and this can help couples to cultivate a healthy balance between the two.

Conclusion

Whilst it is very rare that we go back to the basics of psychology, it is always fun when we do, because we get to learn about key psychological concepts that are the core of our discipline. Therefore, we know that our identity is made up of our values, memories, experiences as well as relationships that make up our sense of self. It is this mixture that creates a steady sense of who we are over time and this remains steady even as new facets of our identity are created. As well as it's important to live authentically because there is a correlation between authenticity and a lot of different aspects of mental health. For example, self-esteem, vitality and coping skills.

And most importantly, living authentically makes us happy.

As a result, at the end of this chapter, let me ask you these questions:

- *What facets is your identity made up of?*
- *What are your values?*
- *How authentically do you live?*

If you answer those questions then you never know where your life, your mental health and choices might lead you. Yet it could make you a lot happier, and isn't that the whole point of life?

THE SELF AND SELF-AWARENESS

The next three chapters serve as a great introduction to the social psychology of the Self, theories of the Self and our Self-Esteem. Also, whilst these chapters are taken from my book *Social Psychology: A Guide To Social and Cultural Psychology*, they're critical to our understanding the science behind these social concepts. As well as this helps us to have a solid foundation of what the Self and our Self-Esteem is before we start exploring the Unshakable Self in more depth in later chapters.

These chapters are a lot of fun, so enjoy.

***

This was the topic that I first learnt about at university after the boring introduction lectures and I have to say that it was very interesting. I hope you enjoy it as well.

Who are we?

Who are you?

These are great questions that are related to the self.

The self is constantly refined because we are constantly refining ourselves.

Personally, I went through a massive refine in March 2019 as I decided to define myself as an author.

In addition, the Self is intrinsically social and the self influences our behaviour.

Interestingly, we tend to view our self-relationships with ourselves like they aren't a part of us. Meaning we view them like an outsider, as well as people can have symbolic relationships with themselves. This is where you view our self-relationships as other people interact with us.

I know that that was extremely complex but imagine as if you're in a room, with yourself as your full being then you see another version of yourself may be sitting on the floor. This other version of you is a version of yourself. This version may be your sad self or lonely self.

I know it's very hard, but it will become clearer as you read on.

Finally, it is very important that we control our behaviour and maintain the self that we want others to see.

<u>Self-Schemas:</u>

As previously mentioned, the Self is made up of different dimensions and can be thought as versions and these dimensions are called schemas.

Schemas are a mental framework that influences how we encode, store and retrieve information.

For more information on schemas, please see Cognitive Psychology.

Furthermore, some schemas are more important than others and you can think of these schemas as parts or dimensions of yourselves. For example, being an author and a psychology student is more important to me than my cooking side.

Therefore, self-schematics are the important parts of the self. Whereas the self aschematic are the less important parts.

<u>Self- Concept and Knowledge:</u>

Whilst these schemas can be about the desired self and undesired self. It must be pointed out that schemas can become all-consuming as the self does influence our daily life.

Meaning if a person has a self-schema about weight. This can lead to excessive weight monitoring.

<u>Self-awareness:</u>

Self-awareness is the psychological state of being aware of your own characteristics, feelings and behaviours. This happens around the age of 18 months.

Public Self-Awareness:

This type of self-awareness is when you have an awareness of the public aspects of yourself, so what other people can see.

This leads to adherence to social norms and society's standards.

However, public self-awareness can be debilitating because of public self-consciousness. This is chronic public self-awareness where a person is too concerned with how they are perceived and evaluated by others.

Private Self-Awareness:

Private self-awareness is an awareness of the private aspect of the self. This can be positive if people focus on positive parts of themselves, but it can be negative, and it can lead to depression if you focus on negative parts of the self.

In my opinion, I am a positive person because I focus on the positive aspects of myself whilst acknowledging the bad as well. For example, I focus on the fact I'm a good psychology student but I'm not the best.

Interestingly, the more self-awareness a person has the more moral and the stronger a person adheres to their own attitudes in general.

The Biological Basis of The Self:

Biologically speaking the self is considered to be created in the anterior cingulate cortex. This is responsible for controlling and monitoring your intention behaviour.

This is because this brain area activates when people become self-aware.

THEORIES OF THE SELF

In social psychology, many theories have been created to explain the self.

Multiple Role Theory:

This recognizes that the self is a very complex thing and it proposes that having multiple selves are important.

It's important because it is a benefit to health and wellbeing to have multiple self-identities. This makes you open to new experiences.

In addition, the theory focuses on both the quality of selves and the quantity.

In my opinion, I think this is a good theory because I know from personal experiences that in order to recover when one of your identities or selves is taken away from you. You need to have other selves to recover.

For example, when something happened to me that made me have to quit scouting. I had to rely on my other selves and refine myself in order to recover. As beforehand my scouting self was a massive part of my overall self, but as I had my author self and a few other selves. I managed to recover. Meaning that my author self replaced the massive hole that my scouting self left behind.

Overall, I hope that that showed you the importance and benefits of having multiple selves.

Self-Perception Theory:

In this theory, Bem, (1967, 1972) argued that people learn about the self by looking at the behaviour that they do as well as by examining their own thoughts, feelings and behaviours.

In my opinion, this is another good theory because I think that we do learn a lot from examining ourselves as we learn what we think and feel about other topics.

On the other hand, later in this book, I will discuss how people aren't as good as they think they are at knowing what they actually think about something.

Self-Discrepancy Theory:

Our next theory is by Higgins (1987) and it focuses on people's attitudes discrepancies between the actual self and the perceived self. These discrepancies can lead to sadness, disappointment and frustration.

Hence, the need for self-regulation as we attempt to match these desired behaviours.

Within this theory, they are several, unique terms that are used to describe the self.

- The actual self- how people perceive the self at a given time.
- The ideal self- how the person would like to perceive themselves.
- The ought self- what the person thinks the self ought to be.

Let's use a personal example of these ideas:

- The actual self- I am a good psychology student that is getting good grades.
- The ideal self and the Ought Self- I want to be a great student that is getting great grades.

As I showed you in the example above sometimes the ideal self and the Ought Self can be the same thing.

Subsequently, if there are discrepancies between the selves then this can lead to different emotional reactions.

Regulatory Focus Theory:

This theory is another theory created by Higgins (1997, 1998) that built upon the self-discrepancy theory to propose people can take two self-regulatory approaches.

The first approach is promotion where people focus on gaining and seeing the ideal self as important. Whereas in the second approach; prevention; people focus on avoiding and preventing as a way to construct the self.

One study on these approaches was a meta-analysis by Bass et al (2008) that found that people with the promotion approach tend to be associated with more creativity.

While the approaches can be changed, they tend to be formed in childhood as promotion focus people tend to have more childhood experiences with an absence or lack of positive adult responses. Whereas prevention focus tends to have a lack of negative adult responses.

Well… personally, I like this theory but I'm a bit unsure about the defining the approaches because I believe that I am either in denial about my childhood having an absence or lack of positive adult responses, or it supports the idea that the theory is making a general claim about promotion people and I'm an outsider.

Whatever, the answer; though I still believe that I'm an outsider; it shows the importance of considering individual differences in psychological theories.

Control Theory of Self-Regulation:

This theory is interesting because this theory explains how people adhere to social norms and societal standards amongst other things.

The theory proposes that people test the self against public and private standards of behaviour. Resulting in them changing their behaviour if there's a discrepancy.

The constant testing of the self allows people to improve the self through self-regulation and self-appraisals.

In addition, people will move into a state of testing and retesting until the discrepancy is resolved.

In other words, if there is a discrepancy between your own behaviour and what the social norm is, then you will constantly change your behaviour until you meet this social norm or standard.

On the other hand, according to the debated theory of ego depletion; this is where the ego and self-control are mental resources that can be used up; self-control cannot be maintained forever. This makes self-control more difficult.

Meaning that people might give up this process of testing and simply deviate from social norms as this is easier.

Social Comparison Theory:

As humans we are all constantly comparing each other to one another, but why do we do this?

People compare themselves to others to validate their dimensions of the self. Yet this is subjective and sometimes unrealistic.

In my life, I have compared myself against friends, family members and even other writers on occasion. Nevertheless, these social comparisons can be completely pointless as we are all different and we all have our own positives and negatives.

To objectively validate ourselves, we take part in:

- Upwards comparison- where people compare themselves to someone who is potentially better at a particular dimension.

Personally, I have compared myself to friends that have had more friendships than me in the past.

- Downward comparison- where people compare themselves to a person who is potentially worse at a given dimension.

I have often compared myself to the other people in my psychology class.

- Temporal comparison- we compare ourselves to a version of ourselves in the past.

I always compare myself to what I was like before something bad happened to me and before I started to take my writing seriously because I'm proud of myself for how far I've come.

Self-Maintenance Model:

This model was created by Tesser (1988) and it focuses on how people maintain self-esteem when faced with upward comparison. Due to upwards comparison can make people feel sad about themselves.

Therefore, when people are faced with these difficulties, people tend to:

- Avoid the comparison person- you avoid the person, so you aren't reminded that they're better than you at something.
- Devalue dimension- you decide that it's not as important as you thought it was.
- Engage in downward comparison- this reminded you that you are better than others at something.
- Exaggeration person's ability- we exaggerate their ability, so we feel that their level is impossible to get to. In turn, this makes us feel better.

SELF-ESTEEM

Self-esteem is very important to have as well as it is a person's subjective appraisals of the self, and it can change a lot. It is constantly moving between high and low self-esteem.

In addition, self-esteem is influenced by upbringing. For example, an authoritarian and permissive parenting style tends to lead to negative self-esteem. Whereas an authoritative style leads to high self-esteem.

<u>Sources of Self-Esteem:</u>

There a lot of sources of self-esteem and we'll investigate them more in a moment. Although I believe that it's important to have a wide range of sources of self-esteem because if one source starts to give us negative self-esteem then the other sources are more likely to cover the negativity. Maintaining positive self-esteem overall.

<u>Sources of Self-Esteem Include:</u>

- Internal- self-esteem depends on self-schemas, emotion and flexibility of evaluations.

In other words, self-esteem can come from what we think of ourselves and we need to be flexible in our evaluation to maintain this self-esteem.

- External sources- this is where sources like social acceptance and other factors are important.
- Sociometer theory- people are motivated to maintain high self-esteem and they do this to ensure they are socially accepted.

<u>Contingent Self-Esteem:</u>

This type of self-esteem is where people base their self-esteem on different factors, because as previously mentioned if self-esteem is based on a wide number of sources then this can lead to high self-esteem. Whereas if self-esteem is based on a narrow number of sources or factors then this tends to decrease self-esteem.

For example, before I was forced to leave scouting, my self-esteem was based on cooking, scouting, writing, Warhammer 40,000, reading, family and friends. Meaning that my self-esteem was based on at least seven factors.

Resulting in when I was forced out and I lost scouting and my friends. I still managed to maintain high self-esteem because I managed to draw my self-esteem from the five remaining factors.

<u>Consequences of Self-Esteem:</u>

Self-esteem has two major impacts on our behaviour because self-esteem can help with our mood regulation as well as it can provide us with Protection From Terror of Death.

This protection is another term for terror management theory and mortality salience. In other words, how terrified we are to know that we WILL die one day.

Additionally, research has found that people with high self-esteem deal with this fear better.

Although, if a person has low self-esteem then they are more likely to be aggressive.

This is because people with lower self-esteem are more terrified knowing that they're going to die. Leading to more aggression.

Finally, narcissistic people have very high self-esteem, but this high esteem comes from an insecure place. Hence, these types of people defend their self-esteem whenever it is questioned.

<u>Self-Presentation:</u>

As humans are very judgmental, everyone is affected by the need to look good or look at least somewhat representable for wider society.

We manage our self-presentation through impression management. This is where we manage the impression you give others, as well as self-monitoring. This is where you control how you present yourself depending on the person and situation.

For example, when I'm alone or just with my immediate family. I typically wear very casual clothes because I don't need to be concerned with self-presentation.

However, when I'm going out and going to my lectures at university. I always wear a pair of jeans in an effort to improve my self-presentation.

Drives for Self-Presentation:

Here are some motives that drive us to strategic self-presentation:

- We want to be liked.
- Make people think we're dangerous
- Makes us be seen as competent
- Makes as morally respectable
- Makes as helpless and in need of sympathy

Accuracy of Self-Knowledge:

As I briefly mentioned earlier, our self-knowledge is limited a lot of the time.

For example, people don't appear to notice when or why their own attitudes change nor do they know how a situation affects their behaviour.

Equally, people don't know why they like things and people believe factors influence their behaviour when they don't influence them.

Moreover, people don't know the extent to which we have free will as well as people have a vested interest in the self.

Finally, people are often affected by the affective forecasting error. This is when we overestimate the emotional impact that positive or negative life events have on us.

In other words, humans are awful at knowing themselves.

Motivated Social Cognition and Self:

Before we dive into this section I wanted to define social cognition.

Social cognition is the subfield of psychology that investigates how people store information that's related to other people and groups, as well as this area looks at the cognitive processes that occur and are involved in social processes.

For example, how a memory about a minor group influences and involved in a social group encounter.

We have several motivations for engaging with our social cognition and exploring the self. For instance:

- We need to find out about a topic.
- We need to have Self-esteem motivation. This acts as self-enhancement.
- Cognitive consistent also known as self-verification.
- Cognitive consistency
- We have a need to affirm control over a situation and this gives us an illusion of control.

Culture and Self:

Our last section will quickly look at Individualism and collectivist cultures. These cultures have a difference in the perception of the importance of distinctiveness, uniqueness and interdependence.

For instance, individualistic cultures would prefer high distinctiveness and interdependence. Whereas a collectivistic culture wouldn't value these characteristics as highly.

Lastly, Bi-cultural people have to deal with different cultures, and they integrate both cultures into the self. This can be challenging but very rewarding as well.

Overall, I hope that you've found it interesting and an enlightening first few chapters.

WHAT MAKES UP THE SELF?

In the last few chapters, we've looked at a lot of the social psychological basics of the Self and in the next chapter, you'll explore the types of Selves that our main Self is made up of. However, in this chapter, I want to focus on the last of the basics of the Self including what makes up the Self, likes its core components, how the self changes throughout our development amongst others.

This is a fascinating chapter and that you are going to enjoy.

What Components Made Up The Self?

The core elements that we're going to be investigating in the first part of this chapter are critical elements that help to make up our individual identities. As well as it is these elements that make us all different and unique from one another.

Firstly, as you'll get reminded about throughout the book, our self-concept is flat out critical in the development of the Self. Our self-concept focuses on how we perceive ourselves. For instance, this includes our social roles, our personality traits as well as our physical attributes amongst others. It is our self-concept that controls our self-perception and it's important to note that our self-perception is not always accurate. Our self-concept is coloured and filtered through our life experiences, our attitudes and the feedback that we receive from others.

For better or for worse.

One way to think about our self-concept not being accurate can be seen in people with depression with their biased cognitive processes about themselves, others and the world. If they got 60% on a test which in UK universities is a 2:1 grade (a very good grade) then the person with depression probably would focus on the 40% and all the topics they didn't get right because they were "silly", "dumb" and "don't deserve to be at university".

Even though they passed the assignment with flying colours.

Secondly, self-efficacy is an important part of the Self because psychologist Albert Bandura coined the term and he was referring to a person's belief in their ability to be successful in a particular task or specific situation. You can think about self-efficacy as your internal cheerleader so you can be confident in tackling whatever challenges you face in life.

As a result when a person has high self-efficacy then we're more likely to see tough tasks as challenges that we need to overcome and master. Whereas if you have low self-efficacy then we can be paralysed, scared and avoid challenging situations, and we could just give up before we even try.

Personally, I have very high self-efficacy

because I know that if I dedicate enough time, learning and commitment then I can overcome any challenge I want within reason. For example, this week I've been dealing with learning Shopify and once you understand it, it is a very easy platform to use and I love it. Yet it was a challenge at first.

Whereas one of my friends has such low self-efficacy that it is painful to see them encounter new challenges because they really do not cope well.

Thirdly, our self-esteem is a core element of the Self as you saw in the last chapter. You already know our self-esteem is focused on how we feel about ourselves. If you have high self-esteem then you can drive yourself towards your goals, you can be confident in who you are and you can help develop your unshakable self.

On the other hand, if you have low self-esteem then you will be filled with doubt and it will hold you back. You might not embrace new opportunities, new challenges and new chances for learning because you will stay within your comfort zone. If we go back to the quote that kicked off this book, it is only by knowing who you are that you'll be able to get rid of your doubts.

Increasing your self-esteem is a large part of this.

And building upon this a little more, after I was raped, as you can expect my self-esteem was nothing. I hated myself with an utter passion but once I'd healed, gone through my rape counselling and I learnt who I was with my core values. I did start to like myself again and it is a great feeling.

Finally, the last core element of the Self is self-awareness. This is your ability to understand and introspect your own emotions, thoughts and behaviours. It allows you to understand how you work and self-awareness is key to personal growth as well as emotional intelligence. It allows you to recognise your own motivations, your strengths and weaknesses, and most importantly, it allows you to make informed choices that align with your goals and values.

When it comes to the message of this book, being able to make decisions that align with who are you is critical for mental health and wider life.

How Does The Self Develop Over The Lifespan?

In this next section of the chapter, you'll develop a firm but brief understanding of how the Self develops over our lifespan. Since in childhood, our sense of self develops at a very early age, such as when we can recognise ourselves in a mirror. Then over time, this sense of self develops further when children are able to see themselves as unique individuals with their own desires, feelings as well as thoughts. During this time, the child's awareness of the Self begins to incorporate more nuanced understanding of their abilities and traits.

In addition, children start to internalise the feedback they receive from their environment and this shapes their early sense of competence and self-worth. For instance, if as a child, someone is criticise for doing basically anything then over time a core element of their sense of self would be low self-worth and competence. They would believe that they are useless at everything.

When it comes to adolescence, I discuss all the social, biological and other cognitive changes in *Developmental Psychology: A Guide To Developmental and Child Psychology* in more depth. Yet for the purposes of this book, the main takeaway is that adolescence is an intense period of identity formation and self-discovery. Adolescents are always struggling with questions about where do they fit in in the world, who are they and so on.

Basically, they struggle with the questions this book aims to answer.

During adolescence, teenagers constantly experiment with different social roles, different beliefs and essentially, they try on different identities like outfits. Therefore, whilst this process of exploration is happening and it can be a very chaotic time in their life, it is critical for the development of a stable sense of self.

It is normally during adolescence that the majority of people find their inner self.

Personally, my adolescence was filled with too much perceived danger, I was too much in fear for my life and so much for me to be able to experiment with identities. Yet during university and in particular, the past two years I have been able to figure out who I am, what I value and the identity that I have created for myself.

When it comes to adulthood, a person's sense of self is a lot more stable because it isn't constantly being changed through the experimentations of teenagers. Yet this doesn't mean that it doesn't change, in fact it really does. We are always refining, developing and reevaluating our sense of self in light of new information that we get from challenging situations. All different life events, be it relationships, parenthood or career changes, they all tell us information that can get us to reconsider who we are as well as what we value.

The sense of self is a constant and, to be honest, never-ending process of integration as we work to maintain a coherent sense of self in amongst the wonderful chaos of life.

Personally, before my healing from my sexual trauma, I thought in friendships I really wanted relationships that we mostly had the same level of deep closeness, and most of my friendships were with people I was romantically attracted to. Yet I learnt during and after I healed from my sexual trauma that actually all I want is kindness and it is okay that not all my friends are going to have the same level of closeness to me as I do with other people.

There are other facets of this thought but that's the general gist. If you're interested in learning more, please check out *Healing As A Survivor.*

Finally, in later life, it is common for people to engage in self-reflection and review their life often. There are times when all of us look back at our life in terms of relationships, achievements and experiences and we integrate them into our cohesive narrative of our self. I talk more about narrative self in the next chapter.

The great benefit of this period in later life is that it is often filled with wisdom and self-acceptance, and we come to terms with finding meaning in our life's journey and the various aspects of our identity.

In my opinion, I would add that if you've experienced a lot of trauma in your life then you do not need to wait for later life to do this self-reflecting and self-acceptance. When this book originally comes out, I'll be 24- and 25 years old, and that is not later life. Yet my trauma and my healing has made me have to reflect on my life experiences and it has made me accept a lot of the different parts of my identity and more just to survive, let alone heal.

As we reach the end of this chapter, here are my questions for you to reflect on and write out an answer to:

- What do you think about yourself?
- How much self-esteem do you have?
- How could you improve your self-esteem?
- Do you have high or low self-efficacy?
- How self-aware are you?

Once you've figured out the answer to those questions, you'll have a clearer idea how to progress with building your unshakable self, and what you could possibly work on.

KNOWING THE QUALITIES YOU LIKE IN PEOPLE

In the last chapter, I got you to start thinking about the importance of finding your values and I gave you a few exercises to help you find your core values. However, I know some people might find that very difficult first of all, so there is an exercise you can do beforehand that might make it easier for you.

After the introductory counselling I had when I started my course of counselling for my anorexia, the first session focused on getting me to think about the positive and negative traits of my friends and family members. The idea behind this exercise was it would allow me to think about what I liked in people. Then this would allow me to know what I look for in friendships and relationships. As well as focusing on other people can be easier to get people thinking about values and traits.

Before you start focusing on yourself.

I'll show you an example for myself first before explaining why this is a very interesting exercise to do.

<u>Positives Of Myself</u>

- Kind
- Friendly
- Supportive
- Intelligent
- Compassionate
- Good listener
- Committed to lifelong learning
- Creative

<u>Negatives Of Myself</u>

- Lack of self-awareness
- Can be obsessive

<u>Positives Of My Best Friend</u>

- Kindness
- Supportive
- Knowledgeable
- Determined
- Funny
- Friendly
- Creative

<u>Negatives Of My Best Friend</u>

- Lack of self-awareness
- At times obsessive

<u>Positives Of Another Close Friend</u>

- Kind
- Funny
- There for others
- Interesting
- Good listener

<u>Negatives Of Another Close Friend</u>

- Lack of self-worthy
- Shy

- Lack of self-esteem

Positives Of Parents

- Kind
- Friendly
- Do not put up with rubbish
- Always there for me
- Supportive

Negatives Of Parents

- Sometimes support feels like an act depending on who's about
- Can't have certain serious talks with them

Whilst those answers are along the lines of what I did in my counselling session even though I know there were some different, I hope you can start to see something interesting. I have a lot of similar traits to my friends, like kindness, supportiveness and so on. As well as a lot of friends share the positive traits of my parents.

Therefore, my counsellor argued that this happens because as children, we internalise what our parents were like and how they behaved, so we seek out people who are similar to them. I think this idea is somewhat true because I have sought out people who are more acceptable and more liberal than my parents, but my friends still share a lot of positive traits of my parents.

Therefore, I wanted to share this little exercise with you because if you're struggling to think about your own values and traits. Then try thinking about the traits of your closest friends, your other friends and your loved ones in terms of the positive and negative traits.

You might be surprised how much overlap there is.

Here are some questions to think about at the end of this chapter after you've done the exercise:

- What traits do me and my friends have in common?
- What traits do me and my parents have in common?
- What traits do my friends and my parents have in common?

Then if you struggled with the exercises in the last chapter, go back and try them now. They might be easier for you.

KNOW YOUR BOUNDARIES

In this chapter, you'll learn why boundaries are critical to building your sense of Self, how to build boundaries and what healthy boundaries look like.

Why Boundaries Help To Build Your Unshakable Self?

When it comes to building your Unshakable Self and knowing who you actually are, a lot of this can be tied back to knowing your boundaries. I think a lot of psychological distress in our lives is created because we don't know our boundaries until it is too late. For example, earlier today, I was writing an anorexia reflection and I explored how me stretching myself too thin and doing what everyone else wanted me to do distressed me so much that my anorexia kicked in. And I didn't eat for 25 hours.

Of course, I know a lot of people who don't have anorexia would find that a bit of an extreme example, but it shows that it isn't helpful to our mental health when we don't stick to our boundaries.

This is even more important to myself personally as a rape survivor. A good chunk of all the distress, trauma responses and depression that came from my Post-Traumatic Stress Disorder came from my boundaries being violated in the worst way possible. This is why I had to learn about boundaries, I had to figure out what my boundaries were and how I was going to reinforce them.

It is because I figured out my boundaries that I was able to feel safe again in my own skin. As well as it is because I set boundaries with my family and loved ones that we were able to develop the brilliant, healthy relationship that we have today.

In addition, because I know my boundaries, I feel empowered about moving forward in my life. For instance, I'm entering a casual relationship so I can explore, learn and have some fun. Yet because I know my boundaries, I know I am in control and I am empowered to protect myself. I compromise with my partner on some things but I will never compromise on some boundaries.

So I am excited about casually dating my partner because it should be a lot of fun and because I know myself, my boundaries and what my limits are, all my doubts, frustrations and fears about the relationship have disappeared.

Ultimately, boundaries are critical to your sense of self, because they help you remain in control. They empower you to make decisions and this is the applied angle of your core values. If your core values are your moral compass then your boundaries are the moral decisions you make to protect yourself, your mental health and what feels right to you.

And knowing your boundaries is a part of knowing who you are.

What Are Boundaries?

Boundaries are what help to protect you from being mistreated as well as boundaries let others know how you want to be treated. They create a healthy emotional and physical space that promotes self-agency. This allows your actions to align with your values instead of doing something because another person wants you to do it.

In an ideal world (and this is what healthy boundaries look like), your boundaries are flexible and elastic because they will shift from one moment to the next and this shift will be intuitive and automatic depending on what you need and what you prefer. For instance, as a baseline, I have no problem hugging my friends. Yet if I was very vulnerable and if my mental health wasn't the best there would be certain friends I wouldn't want a hug from and there was certain friends I would really, really want a hug from. And if I was really stress then I probably wouldn't want a hug at all.

It just depends on what I need and prefer at that moment in time.

Nonetheless, the issue is a lot of us where never really taught healthy boundaries as children. We were taught boundaries by our parents or our primary caregiver because they set boundaries on us to protect us from the world. Such as, don't run in the street, don't run away in a shopping mall, don't do this, don't do that and so on.

Therefore, we know this was to keep us safe but we had no choice, no control and we didn't understand as children whether you were modelled healthy boundaries or not. So whilst children have to be given limits, the issue is a lot of children are shamed without repair or they are punished as they try to assert healthy boundaries.

I know I was always punished as a child if I rebelled or tried to place limits on activities that were harming my mental health. For instance, when my family was being extremely homophobic, I was shamed and punished for trying to put these boundaries in place.

As a result, often children have to put walls around themselves to survive and adapt or they have to learn what other people want at the expense of taking care of themselves. This is what I did throughout my childhood and adolescence. I always focused on surviving, keeping other people happy and just doing everything I could so I had options if people found out I was gay and they wanted to beat me, kick me out or kill me.

In addition, other people might have felt responsible for the happiness of a family member or loved one so they might have learnt to ignore their own limitations, needs and desires so they could focus on making someone happy.

Ultimately, all boundaries, including healthy and unhealthy ones, are survival tools that we use at some point in our lives. Yet the issue is if we don't learn to set healthy boundaries then we will pay a price. I know the price I paid because I didn't set boundaries with my family was they kept walking over me, I kept acting scared and getting distressed and it only harmed my mental health.

And my rape recovery.

What To Do Moving Forward?

On the whole, moving forward, you need to learn to set healthy boundaries with a clear *yes* or *no*. Since if you don't then you risk feeling coerced and used even if other people don't intend to take advantage of you and they would normally respect your boundaries (Odgen and Fisher, 2015).

Lastly for this section, you being able to set boundaries is critical to feeling a sense of empowerment. Also, learning to say no with your words and body can be difficult at first, and it is common to feel guilt and shame, but you will find relief in no longer doing things you don't want to do.

Personally, this is something I found when I started to say no to driving my housemates as much as I used to. It was nice not running round after everyone else, and I was actually able to focus on what I wanted for me. This meant I could do what made me happy instead of trying to make everyone else happy for a change.

It was lovely.

What Types of Boundaries Exist?

I know within society when people think about boundaries, this largely comes back to sexual boundaries, but even though sexual boundaries are flat out critical. There are more boundaries out there.

For example, physical boundaries include things like your personal space as well as physical touch. Like you and you alone get to decide how close someone can get to you and how much alone and privacy you get. For me, I don't like people too close to me unless it's my partner, so I make sure everyone stays back at a comfortable distance.

Whereas intellectual boundaries, which I had never heard of before my rape, are boundaries around our thoughts and ideas. For instance, it isn't okay for people to criticize you, your thoughts and your ideas, or for someone to take credit for them.

This is something I have never allowed.

In addition, when it comes to material

boundaries, these are boundaries around your possessions and money. Like it is your right to be paid for your time at your job for your work and you choose whether to loan people money or not.

This is something I did early on with my best friend because I was trying to learn boundaries more. Therefore, once when we were going to go climbing and they couldn't pay, I said no to paying for them. It felt good because we still hung out and it meant that my best friend knew I wasn't the type to give them money all the time. Even though they are not that sort of person who would ask for that.

Another type of boundary is time and I am very hot on this type these days. Since boundaries around your time involve demands on and how you choose to spend your time. Only you have the right to choose not to let other people convince you to do something you don't want to do, only you get to decide if you do any unpaid work, as well as you have the right to dedicate time to self-care.

Personally, in recent months, I am really focusing more on my time boundaries. For my mental health and my happiness, I need to have enough time to do everything I want to do in my business, my writing and social life. If I do too much university work or too much Outreach work then this puts too much demand on my time and I am the one that suffers.

Also, this is why I don't mind the idea of a casual relationship because me and my partner can do all our different projects, spend time with our friends and we still get to go on dates and do fun things a few times a week without having to spend all our time together.

On the other hand, you have sexual boundaries too. These are boundaries you place around whether a partner or loved one can touch you, where you're okay with them touching you and the quality of that touch.

I know for me personally these are very firm boundaries, because without going into details. I need to have the rape conversation with my partner because I am more than happy to have sex with them but we are going to have to be careful. Also, there are two body parts that my rapist loved more than anything so I probably won't allow my partner to touch those areas for a little while and these are boundaries I will communicate to protect myself and my mental health.

Finally, you have non-negotiable boundaries, there are boundaries that you absolutely have to have in order to feel safe. A lot of these non-negotiable boundaries can come from the other categories too. Such as, you have the right to walk away when someone has betrayed you and your trust by breaking a boundary or an agreement. For me, I would walk away from a relationship if I asked my partner not to touch a certain body part and they keep repeatedly doing it against my wishes.

I would definitely walk because I am not going through what I went through that night ever again.

What Are Healthy Boundaries?

Our boundaries can be rigid, porous or flexible and healthy. If you keep losing people or you tend to avoid them by keeping them at a distance, then you have very rigid boundaries. Since when people have overly rigid boundaries then people tend to be unlikely to ask for help, seem detached even with their romantic partners, keep others at a distance out of fear of rejection, avoid close relationships and intimacy and are overly protective of personal information.

Whereas if you have porous boundaries then this is where you tend to get overly involved through oversharing personal information, having difficulty saying no to other people, be overly involved in other people's problems, complying with other people out of fear of rejection and being dependent on the opinions of others.

Or you can have healthy boundaries where you don't tend to overshare or under share personal information, you value your own opinions, you are accepting when other people say no, you accept and acknowledge your own personal wants and needs, as well as you never compromise your values for other people.

Ultimately, whilst you'll have a preference for one type of boundary, you will probably have a mix of healthy, porous and rigid depending on how you're feeling at a given time, what situation you are in and how you feel about the people or person you are with. If you have healthy boundaries then you can say no to other people when you choose to as well as you're comfortable to open up to intimacy and close relationships when you want to.

Conclusion

There are a lot of exercises that you can find out about online that will help you to understand and find your boundaries. However, I want to stress here that boundaries are so important to finding yourself and who you are. Because once you know your boundaries, then this gives *you* control in your life and it empowers *you* to know what will make you happy and what will not.

Also, once you know your boundaries, your doubts, fears and frustrations about a given situation will disappear. For me, because I know what boundaries are and what I will do not do in a relationship or a partner, I am not as scared as I was because about starting or exploring something new. I am the one in control and that's exciting, and that is only because I know my boundaries and who I am.

Hopefully, once you know your boundaries, you'll have the same freedom.

Here are my questions for you at the end of this chapter:

- How were boundaries modelled to you as a child?
- How might healthier boundaries been modelled to you?
- What current situations have you wanted to say no to but you didn't feel able to?
- What are your boundaries in terms of
- Physical
- Intellectual
- Sexual
- Material
- Time
- Non-negotiable

WHERE DID YOUR SELF COME FROM?

After you experience trauma, especially if it is sexual trauma or another form of "short", sharp trauma (my other example of trauma lasted for a decade so anything is short to me in comparison), it feels like you've lost a part of yourself and your sense of self has been attacked and violated.

Before you can ever hope to find out who

you are, and I mean who you *actually* are beyond the trauma and pain and abuse, you need to understand how does trauma and abuse impact your sense of self.

This chapter is a great starting point for that because if you've been a long-term listener or reader of my psychology books or podcast then you might be aware that I've experienced childhood and sexual trauma in my life.

As you can imagine this had had a wide range of negative impacts on my Self. For example, my trauma has meant I have Post-Traumatic Stress Disorder, anxiety, abandonment issues and I have a lot of friendship difficulties, partly because of autism, partly because of friendship trauma too. Equally, I've lived with other traumatised housemates at university and I can see how trauma impacts someone's sense of self. But how? Therefore, in this chapter, you'll learn how does trauma and abuse impact sense of self, how can we heal a survivor's sense of self and more.

How Does Trauma and Abuse Impact Sense of Self?

I've spoken a lot about the mental health impact of trauma and abuse on the podcast before but today I want to focus on how it impacts our sense of self. As a result of any kind of abuse and trauma is an attack on our sense of self. It doesn't matter if a person controls or abuses us through words or actions, the result is the same. It devalues us and it elevates the abuser. Therefore, if you've experienced emotional abuse in the past, like I have, or if you're experiencing it at the moment then you should never ever accept it, deny it, ignore it or perpetuate it.

The abuse will continue to pervasively and destructively attack your sense of self.

In addition, abuse tends to have the following negative impacts on our sense of self:

- Increased loneliness
- Lack of self-confidence
- Low self-esteem
- Transfer of needs
- Failure Syndrome
- Perfectionism
- Acting out sexually
- Unresolved resentments and anger
- Crisis oriented
- Unrealistic guilt

Personally, my abuse caused me a lot of loneliness, because it is hard to accept and connect with other gay people when you were abused and in fear for your life every single day for being gay. As well as because I was so isolated through my abuse where I wasn't really allowed any of my own friends, and this was compounded by my undiagnosed autism, life was very lonely. Also, even before I was raped, I had very low self-esteem because I was always being moaned and shouted at as a kid so I was never really able to feel good about myself. As well as I understand transfer of needs.

And ultimately, I am slightly better at this now but I still have a long way to go, but I was absolutely terrified to make a mistake in a friendship. I would get extremely, extremely distressed if someone told me I had made a mistake despite it being perfectly natural for great friends to bump heads. Yet because of my childhood and past friendships, a mistake meant big trouble for me.

As a result, countering the lies that emotional abuse gets a survivor to believe is important, because we need the survivor to understand their true nature and their values. This means we need them to believe in their true value, to reject the lies of their emotional victimisation, as well as we need to help them learn more about their true self and not their abused self.

Ultimately, it is about helping our client commit to exchanging the negative effects of emotional abuse with more positive and affirming characteristics.

Personally, I'll admit this is very hard and it is something I am still learning. I am still learning how to have healthy friendships, relationships and how not to get extremely distressed whenever I make a mistake. Also, I am learning how to like me for me and how to live in an environment where I am not in fear for my life, where I am not scared of being killed and where I can just be all of me without fear.

That is taking a long time to get used to, but I am getting there slowly and I'm grateful for my friends for putting up with me in the meantime. And I am grateful for the boundaries that I have put in place and I am reinforcing them with my family and it is wonderful to see how great our relationship is these days, and I love them more than ever.

My takeaway questions at the end of this chapter are:

- Is abuse and trauma impacting your sense of self?
- And if so, how is it impacting your sense of self?
- How could you change your sense of self for the better?

WHAT IS INTERNAL FAMILY SYSTEMS THERAPY?

Whilst it is mainly in other books, I talk about different forms of psychological therapy and they can help people to decrease their psychological distress, improve their lives and find more adaptive ways of coping with stressors, I want to talk about Internal Family Therapy for a very specific reason. The entire point of this book is to show you how you might build your Unshakable Self and Internal Family Therapy can help us do this by offering us an interesting way to look at the Self.

The therapy is filled with a lot of fascinating ideas that we can use, adapt and pull on when thinking about how to make our Selves stronger, more resilience and more unshakable. I hope you enjoy this chapter as much as I do.

What Is Internal Family Therapy?

To my utter shock and amazement, this actually has nothing to do with families and the systemic approach to mental health. I honestly believed this was another type of family therapy but it turns out this therapy is completely different.

Therefore, Internal Family Systems Therapy is a form of psychotherapy that focuses on identifying and addressing the different families or sub-personalities within a client's mental system. And yes, please bear with me because this does sound woo-woo but I think this is actually an interesting idea that I have personal experience with, so please keep reading.

These sub-personalities are made up of the different wounded parts of our Self as well as the painful emotions, like shame and anger, that form a person. In addition, to the parts of the Self that try to protect and control us from the pain caused by the wounded parts of us.

Then similar to traditional psychodynamic theory, these different parts are often in conflict with each other and our Core Self. The idea of the Core Self is this is the part of us that is compassionate, confident and represents all of us, and this is within everyone.

As a result, Internal Family Systems Therapy focuses on healing our wounded parts as well as restoring our mental balance and harmony by helping the client to change the dynamics creating the discord between these families of mental systems and the Self.

Furthermore, Internal Family Systems Therapy was developed by a family therapist called Richard Schwartz who found patterns in how people described their inner lives. Therefore, he started to form the idea that the mind was a family and contained different family members that interacted with each other, and the exploration of these different family members and how they functioned was the foundation of Internal Family Therapy.

I'll give my own personal thoughts on this "theory" that clearly isn't empirically backed in a moment, because I like the theory and the description. I just cannot see it has any research support.

How Does Internal Family Systems Therapy Work?

When it comes to how the therapy works, Internal Family Systems Therapy focuses on the idea that the undamaged core Self is who a person really is. Also, the therapy works by healing and transforming the wounded parts of the Self, and this allows the Core Self to better manage these other parts.

This is done by achieving the three goals of Internal Family Therapy. Firstly, a client and therapist work together to free the wounded parts from their extreme roles. Secondly, a client needs to restore trust in the Self and finally, a client needs to harmonise and coordinate between the Core Self and the different parts. This allows them all to work together as a team with the Core Self (remember this is who the client actually is) in charge.

My Personal Thoughts On Internal Family Systems Therapy From A Theoretical Standpoint

I hate that I'm in two minds about the theory this therapy is based on.

Firstly, as an aspiring clinical psychologist that firmly believes in the scientist-practitioner model of clinical practice, I hate this theory. This isn't based on any research, any studies, anything close to science. This theory is based on the observations of a therapist without being tested in any empirical setting and I have no doubt there have been studies since its creation testing it out. But considering how fringe this therapy is in academic settings and even in clinical settings I haven't really seen this used at all, I think that little fact further stresses how unempirical this theory is.

However, as someone who went through a mental breakdown in August 2023 and went for private therapy in the same month. I hate to say that I largely agree with this theory from a personal viewpoint to some extent. Since during my own therapy sessions, I did describe my Self as bunch of different parts that didn't always see eye to eye but largely they were integrated together.

Except for the gay part of my Self which was subjected to a decade of abuse, trauma and intense threats. I always described that part of my Self as a 16 year old teenager that was scared, isolated and always expecting to die.

That was a useful concept to use in therapy because it made my point very clear and it was something to work with. And something she suggested was I talk to that damaged, scared part of my Self to see what they needed, what I wanted to say to it and try to fully integrate it into the rest of my Self.

I ended up writing a letter or two to this part of my Self anyhow.

I know that is somewhat different to what Internal Family Systems Therapy is saying but it did help me. I know not everyone would find it useful but I did and now I know that part of my Self isn't 16 year old teenager that's scared. That Gay part of my Self is just a small part of me now like the rest of my Self is.

Interestingly, this actually has a name and this is a 6-step process of Internal Family Systems Therapy that helps a client to identify the different parts of their Self and release the burdens that these Parts carry.

1. The therapist helps the client identify the part of the Self that needs attention.
2. The client focuses attention to the relevant part.
3. The client fleshes out this Part by describing it and what their experience of it is.
4. The client explores how the feel towards this part of the Self.
5. They express curiosity towards the part and accept its presence.
6. The client asks what this part fears and what it would fear if the role for it changed.

That's what I did with the letter to the Gay traumatised part of myself.

Overall, I think in clinical psychology, we can be and I think we need to be snobbish and arrogant about making sure our clinical practice is focused on science and research. Yet we still should be aware of other less-empirical ideas at times just in case we ever meet a client that might find things useful. As clinical psychologists, 99% of our practice has to be based on research and science, I will never doubt that, but awareness of any therapy doesn't hurt.

<u>When Is Internal Family Systems Therapy Used?</u>

I'm glad to see that my belief in Internal Family Systems Therapy being used to treat families wasn't completely wrong, because the therapy can be used to treat couples, families and individuals experiencing a wide range of mental health conditions as well as symptoms. For instance:

- Panic
- Anxiety
- Depression
- Substance use
- Physical health conditions, like arthritis
- General functioning and well-being
- Trauma

Nonetheless, Internal Family Systems Therapy isn't for everyone because it probably isn't useful for clients with severe mental health conditions that involve paranoia and psychosis. Due to it might be harmful or unproductive to say these clients have different "parts" of themselves.

In terms of research, there is some support for Internal Family Therapy. For instance, in 2015 it was named an evidence-based practice on the National Registry for Evidence-Based Programmes in the USA. As well as one study found that Internal Family Systems Therapy was effective in treating depression in a sample of young women and a small randomised control trial found the therapy helps clients with pain, depressive symptoms, physical functioning amongst other symptoms.

However, my point still remains because Internal Family Systems Therapy doesn't have the strong research base that other psychotherapies do.

What To Expect From Internal Family Systems Therapy?

Like all other psychotherapies, Internal Family Systems Therapy is a talking therapy where a client works with a therapist to find and understand the specific families or sub-personalities that make up a person's mental system. Then after these parts have been identified, the therapist works with the client to acknowledge their feelings about these suppressed emotions, so the client can release these feelings. This makes the client free to address the actual problem and ultimately, it helps the client to find more positive ways to manage the conflict on their way in the future. These more positive ways might include relaxation, keeping a reflective journal, exercise, visualisation or even creating a chart that shows the relationship between the different parts of them and the Core Self.

Moreover, there are a range of different models to help support Internal Family Systems Therapy, including a model that proposes the different parts of the Self have one of three different roles to play for a client.

Firstly, there are Manager parts. These are the protective parts of the Self that control a client's surroundings, manage their emotions and help a client to navigate their daily life.

Secondly, there are what are known as Exile parts. These are the parts of the Self that are filled with the shame, fear or hurt caused by our early experiences and they carry the difficult memories and emotions associated with these experiences. Therefore, it is the job of the Manager parts to keep these Exile Parts contained and hidden from our conscious awareness so we aren't in distress and emotional hurt.

That paragraph really resonated with me.

Finally, there are Firefighter parts. These parts of the Self become activated whenever the Exile parts make us feel any painful, threatening or overwhelming emotion by doing this by any means necessary. Hence, why people partake in substance abuse, binge eating, excessive drinking and a whole host of other maladaptive coping mechanisms.

As a result, if we take me as a good example, my Exile Parts held the pain associated with my trauma, abuse and shame. All these feelings were suppressed by the Manager and the Firefighter Parts engaged in self-harm, extreme dieting and partial suicidality.

Thankfully none of that happens now because of therapy.

Finally, Internal Family Systems Therapy proposes that all of us have a core Self that represents who we really are, that is waiting to be accessed. Then the Self can identify, watch and help these other parts of the Self to become less extreme, more productive and coexist more effectively.

Part of this is that the Self has a lot of good traits that include what's known as the 8 Cs and the five Ps. The entire point of these letters is to help us understand how much of the Core Self is available to a client at a given point in time and how much the Self remains hidden.

As a result, the 8 Cs are:

- Calmness
- Confidence
- Creativity
- Curiosity
- Clarity
- Compassion
- Connectedness
- Courage

With the 5 Ps being:

- Patience
- Presence
- Perspective
- Persistence
- Playfulness

On the whole, in Internal Family Systems Therapy, these letters are useful in helping a therapist to understand how much work they have to do with a client, and how many parts they need to identify to help the client's Core Self emerge. Therefore, allowing the client to finally be with their genuine Self without all these warring, conflicting Parts of the Self.

Conclusion

Overall, Internal Family Systems Therapy is a form of psychotherapy that focuses on identifying and addressing the different families or sub-personalities within a client's mental system. And as much as I would love to say this therapy is woo-woo and it doesn't have too much of a place in modern clinical psychology, I'm actually not. Don't get me wrong, I fully believe we should focus on more empirically backed forms of psychotherapy and Internal Family Systems Therapy is far, far from perfect, but it is useful at times.

I know from my own therapy sessions, Internal Family Systems Therapy (which I didn't know my therapist was drawing on) that it is very useful and it allows me to stand here in my audio booth without emotional pain and without trauma and abuse holding me back.

So if you're an aspiring or qualified psychologist, I would say think about what you've read in this chapter, see if anything resonates with you and maybe store away a technique or two just in case you ever want to use it in your practice. Nothing on the book is ever any sort of official advice but it doesn't mean you cannot learn something for the future, for yourself or for the amazing clients that walk through your doors.

WHAT TYPES OF SELF MAKE UP YOUR SELF?

I'll mention how this can help people with trauma build or rebuild their sense of self in a moment. Yet in the last chapter, I introduced you to the idea of Internal Family Systems because it raised an interesting point about how the different types and facets of our Self are together like a family. They are different facets of the Self that interact, combine and when building our sense of Self, it is important that they are all united.

Of course, I will be the first to admit that this has no evidence behind it and it is not empirical at all. Therefore, this is not a good psychological concept and certainly does not represent the rest of psychology. Yet I am a believer in the idea that sometimes when it comes to psychoeducational concepts, they do not need to be 100% accurate if it helps laypeople understand psychological concepts in a therapeutic sense.

Internal Family System is useful in that

regard so I don't mind it too much. For example, when I was having my rape counselling, the way how my rape counsellor explained trauma responses in the brain was not accurate, but as a survivor, it was useful and it helped me start the therapeutic process.

Anyway, now that you understand one idea about the Self in the sense that the Self is made up of different facets that come together to form our Self. I want to use this chapter to break down the types of Self make up you and me.

Personally, I like to think of these types of beliefs as broad categories that can include single versions of the Self or multiple if you will.

Let's start exploring.

Furthermore, I should note that these focuses on the Self can be very useful for people who have experienced trauma and are trying to build or rebuild their sense of self.

What You Belief About You

This focus of the Self involves questions about what do you believe about yourself, what are your attributes and what are your qualities. If you remember earlier in the book then you might have done those exercises that help you to think about these questions.

Nonetheless, these questions are hard. Especially, after trauma because our mind tends to be elsewhere. After my rape, my mind was always on keeping me safe, watching for danger and just staying alive.

Instead, you can ask yourself what others (especially people who like and care about you) believe about you and then affirming those beliefs about yourself too. For example, during the worst mental health impacts of my sexual trauma, I was questioning if I was trying hard enough, if I was being silly, if I was a bad person, etc.

When it comes to us thinking about ourselves, it is important that we solve questions and any tension that we have about our Self by inquiring, affirming and accepting compassionately that the Self is complex. For example, if you question if you are a good person or not then you will have to think about and probably admit, that 99% of the time you are a great person. Yet there is 1% of the time when you are not and that's okay. That's normal and it makes you human.

Ultimately, some people argue that what you believe about your Self is only a single aspect of the Self. It is an important part with a lot of mental health implications but if you build the other parts of the Self too that I will mention in a moment then this will help. It will help you to balance what other people think about you with what you think about yourself.

What Do You Believe About the World

The first two focuses of the Self really do follow on from Beck's theory of depression with the cognitive triad with negatively biased beliefs about the Self, Others and the World.

This focus of the Self involves questions about do you see the world as mostly agnostic and hostile or is it kind and gentle? And how does this worldview impact the expression of your identity?

Personally, whilst I largely believe the world is a good place filled with good people and I subscribe to the idea that humanity is 51% good and 49% bad. I was abused as a child with an extremely homophobic upbringing so I will always be biased and believe that I am not allowed to be openly gay in case I am beaten and killed. I am learning to be better but it is still a worldview that negatively impacts my ability to express my identity.

Equally, when my mental health was at its worst after my sexual trauma, I didn't quite believe that the world was extremely dangerous, but I do remember constantly being terrified of being raped again. It certainly made me scared of the world.

On the whole, when it comes to trauma, we need to remember that we are more than our opinions and it is important that we relate correctly to the world.

So ask yourself:

- What are your beliefs about the world?
- How do they impact the expression of your Self?

The Narrative Sense of Self

This third focus of the Self involves thinking about the journeys in your life of belonging, meaning, wellness and identity. For instance, what are your invisible and visible identities, what needs to be affirmed, what is still oppressed, hidden or suppressed? Where do you feel like you do and do not belong? And so on.

You can practice these questions by picking one of your values from earlier, writing about why it is important and then some places where it has and hasn't been present in your life. As well as afterwards, you can write down some ways to cultivate it in your life.

I did a version of this towards the end of my rape counselling and then a month later. In January 2025, I really thought about all the things that were important to me and I just hadn't been able to do in 2024 because of my sexual trauma. All the things I listed really came back to creativity so that's why in 2025, I have really focused on cultivating this facet of my Self through reading, writing and a whole host of other projects.

Ultimately, if you want to build or rebuild yourself, you need to consider where does cultivating this value takes you on those journeys of belonging, meaning, wellness and most importantly, identity?

The Relational Sense of Self

Fourthly, we need to acknowledge that a large part of our sense of Self comes from who we are to other people. Due to you can ground yourself in service to others, like experiences of caring and being cared about can bring us back into ourselves.

In practical terms, this means you can practice sending "loving kindness phrases" to others, even strangers (even though I am so not brave enough to try that) with some examples including:

- May you be filled with loving kindness
- May you be happy
- May you be well
- May you be at peace and at ease

Interestingly enough, researchers have found that directing these types of phrases at people, including strangers, for a few minutes can boost our subjective sense of well-being. I suppose this makes sense because we are being nice to other people and this makes us feel good in turn.

Therefore, the takeaway from this type of Self is to think about who we are to other people, and try to be kind to others so they see us as a kind person too who wants to care about us as much as we care about them.

Experiential Sense Of Self

The fifth type of Self is the experiential sense of self and this is your present-centred inner experience of your feelings, moods, emotions, suffering and thoughts. And whilst it is the most intangible of the facets of Self that we'll cover in this chapter, it is still important.

We can stabilise our inner experience with self-compassion and mindfulness.

Below is a section from my book *Healing As A Survivor* because I want to talk you through with an example how you can add some self-compassion into your life, and this seriously works.

Self-Compassionate Steps

This was a critical part of my own healing journey because I have never been very self-compassionate but once you realise it is okay to show compassion to yourself. Your life will change forever in a very, very good way and it takes a little bit of time to practise but it is a great technique to use.

Therefore, Doctor Kristin Neff developed the following five steps to help you become self-compassionate:

1. Understand shame is normal and it doesn't need to be eliminated. It is okay to feel shame.

2. Acknowledge you are hurting and you are distressed.

3. Understand other people go through the same thing.

4. Pretend you're talking to a dear friend that is going through the same thing as you. What would you say to them?

5. Say that to yourself and take it in. Internalise what you would say to a dear friend.

Be your friend for a change. Treat yourself as you would a friend, never treat yourself as an enemy.

So to use these self-compassionate steps with the PTSD example at the birthday celebration, I would:

1. Acknowledge that I was distressed about being in a large group, having to support myself as much as I could and I was hurting that my best friend was in a relationship with someone who wasn't me.

2. It's okay to feel like this because other people hurt when people who they are interested in are no longer available, and lots of other survivors experience anxiety.

3. I would ensure my dear friend that it's okay to feel like this. It doesn't make them a bad person, a bad friend and it doesn't make them weak. It just means they are a survivor of something awful and they are healing. They can come down whenever they want, they can choose to stay upstairs and they do whatever they need to do. Because they are important too.

4. And I would say that to myself and accept it, because it is all true.

Self-compassion often requires practice but it is so important.

The Cultural Sense of Self

Our sixth focus of the Self focuses on what is your sense of identity and self in your culture? What's your demographic identity, what is your relationship to your humanity, what alienates you and connects you? How do you cultivate a connection to something bigger than yourself?

For instance, at the time of writing, I'm a 23-year-old white British non-binary person who's gay. Some things that alienate me includes racism, hate, homophobia and transphobia. I connect to something larger than myself by wanting to help make the world a better place so that's why I write, I podcast and I want to add a little more beauty and knowledge into the world.

Jeremiah Brent, an American interior designer, mentioned on one of his programmes once that his mother used to say something along the lines of *we need to leave the world more beautiful than we found it.*

That is what I want for humanity. I want the world to be a better place when I die than when I was born.

What are your answers for those questions?

The Bodily Sense of Self

If you've read *Healing As A Survivor* then you should be aware that in trauma work, the body is very important. Therefore, our bodies are a very grounded and concrete part of our Self and our identity. Since after experiencing trauma, our emotions and mind go in a thousand different directions that are extremely distressing, so a large part of trauma work is rebuilding your sense of bodily identity.

Personally, it took me months upon months to feel safe in my own house living with my dear friends who I logically knew would never ever hurt me. My body sometimes felt so alien to me that it was like I wasn't in it and other times I was so extremely aware of my own body that my PTSD would be so bad. This was the body I was raped in and I did not want to be in it.

I wanted a new body after my rape so I hated my bodily sense of Self with an extreme passion.

As a result, to build or rebuild your bodily sense of self you can ground yourself using grounding techniques. I really recommend the 5-Steps to Mindfulness. Which is a very good technique focusing on getting you to name 5 things you see, 4 things you can touch, 3 things you can hear, 2 or 1 things you can smell and taste. That helps you to ground yourself in the present moment instead of any trauma memories or flashbacks or trauma responses you're experiencing.

There are a lot of other ones that I like but that is a very easy one to get you started with, but just look it up online for more.

Conclusion

Ultimately, in this chapter, we've looked at a lot of different aspects of the Self and there are a lot of areas we can focus on when trying to build or rebuild our unshakable self. As part of my own trauma healing and recovering from my anorexia, I've had to really focus on my Self and really think about who I am.

I really hope that this chapter has given you a lot of questions and areas to think about, because once you answer these questions, you'll be closer to realising who you really are.

WHAT IS SELF-WORTH?

Out of all the different concepts centred around the Self, your self-worth might be the most important. Your self-worth determines how you interact with others, how you perceive the world and it heavily influences your mental health. Therefore, by the end of this chapter, you'll learn what is self-worth, why is self-worth so important to our mental health and how can you improve self-worth.

What Is Self-Worth?

Self-worth is essentially how you feel about yourself in terms of believing you are a good person and you are worthy enough to be treated with respect. Also, self-worth means you value yourself.

You might think self-worth is the same as

self-value but according to Stosny (2014) self-value is "more behavioural than emotional, more about how you act toward what you value including yourself, than how you feel about yourself compared to others".

In addition, self-esteem is slightly different to self-worth especially for people who don't live and breathe concepts of the Self and academically study these concepts. Instead self-esteem is different to self-worth because of the following quote from Hibbert (2013), "self-esteem is what we think and feel and believe about ourselves. Self-worth is recognising 'I am greater than all of those things'. It is a deep knowing that I am of value, that I am loveable, necessary to this life, and of incomprehensible worth."

Personally, as I read that quote again I felt a strange emotion wash over me. Maybe I was doubting that I have high self-worth because the words "that I am loveable" really hit me, because the concept of being loveable connects a lot to my childhood trauma and my rape. In essence, it is not uncommon for rape survivors to feel broken and unlovable and even now those feelings pop up from time to time.

Yet that is the difference between self-esteem and self-worth.

Ultimately, our self-worth is important because it is core to who we are. Every behaviour, every thought, every feeling is tied to how we view our value and our worth as a person.

<u>What Is Self-Worth Theory?</u>

Self-worth theory proposes that a person mainly wants to find self-acceptance in their life and this comes from their achievements (Covington and Beery, 1976). Often these achievements can be found through competing with other people, because competition helps us to feel like we have impressive achievements. Then this makes us feel proud of ourselves and this enhances our self-acceptance.

In addition, the Self-worth Theory believes there are four elements that make up our self-worth. These are our effort, ability, performance and self-worth with the first three interacting together to determine a person's level of worth. Then a person's amount of effort and their ability has a big impact on their performance so this has a knock-on effect on their self-worth and value.

Personally, I really don't like this theory because whilst this model is sort of how we experience feelings of self-worth. It actually focuses way too much on achievements and as I'll explain in a moment, there are a lot more factors that determine our self-worth than simply competing and winning against other people. For example, our social circle determines our self-worth because some people judge their own value based on their social status, and if they know any influential or important people.

In a way, before I understood the concept of the Self and how it applied to my mental health as well as before I improved my self-esteem. I used to get distressed by the idea of not having a lot of friends or at least not a lot of "going out" friends. People who I could go out with instead of texting. Yet since I've increased my self-worth and realise how I am a pretty great person, this isn't as distressing for me anymore because I do have a lot of friends.

Our career and what we do is another factor that determines our self-worth because we often judge other people for what they do. For instance, we tend to believe that a banker is more successful than a builder or cleaner.

Another factor is our net worth, so this means that our material possessions, financial and mean income can determine our self-worth.

Penultimately, our physical appearance can determine our self-worth because some people determine their worth by the size of their clothing, their waistline, their weight amongst other factors.

Finally for this first chapter on self-worth, a lot of people, myself included, determine their self-worth based on what they achieve like I mentioned earlier. Personally, I do this because I flat out love being productive and my mental health always starts to tip when I am not being productive or doing the tasks that I want to do. For example, when I overbook myself doing Student Ambassador work at my university this stops me from doing the psychology, writing and business tasks that I flat out love, so this decreases my mental health.

These tasks are how I relax and do self-care so I need to focus and make sure I do them.

There are other factors that determine our self-worth but those are the main five factors.

My question at the end of this chapter seems very simple but it will get you thinking:

- List all the things that your self-worth is based on, and note down if they are external (not in your control) or internal (you control them).

HOW DO YOU IMPROVE YOUR SELF-WORTH?

Now that we know why self-worth is so important to our mental health, we need to understand how we foster that in ourselves and others so they can experience the benefits of having high self-worth. When it comes to adults, you can increase self-worth by focusing and learning about the things that do not determine your self-worth. For example, how much money is in your bank account, your job title, your relationship status, basically anything external does not determine your self-worth. Instead you need to look at what actually matters to you and you should think about what really determines someone's self-worth. This includes your kindness, your empathy, compassion, respect for others and how well you treat other people.

These factors actually determine self-worth, not your money and other external factors that you don't control.

Another way you can increase your self-worth is to work on identifying, externalising and challenging your inner critic. This is the inner "voice" according to Firestone (2014) that likes to point out our flaws and nitpick about everything we do. Like everyone, I allow my inner critic to win sometimes but if it wins too much then we start feeling awful about ourselves. This goes back to the example about me having major issues with making mistakes in social relationships. My inner critic loves to torment me about my mistakes and how people have left me in the past because of my mistakes. I used to always let my inner critics win so I hated myself because of my negative self-image. Now I don't let it get to me as much and I challenge my inner critic on its irrelevant and warped points, and I'm better for it.

Moreover, when it comes to improving self-worth in adolescents, it's about encouraging them to understand and accept their own self-worth. With self-worth in this context being a value or skill instead of something they need to "do" so they know they need to value themselves for who they are, not what they do.

This led Clark-Jones (2012) to recommend two main strategies to help improve self-worth in adolescents. Firstly, you need to show them unconditional respect, positive regard and love because this helps them to understand it's okay to love yourself for who you are and what they are instead of loving them for what they achieve in an effort to earn your love and respect. If you make a teenager earn love, respect and positivity then they'll put less emphasis on their own self-respect and self-love. This will only lead to a negative self-image over time.

Personally, there were a few situations or aspects of my Self that were never shown positive regard, unconditional love or respect for as a child. It's why for so many years I have struggled with self-worth and actually admitting that I am a great person. It probably was the source of my bad mental health for years before my trauma healing.

Secondly, you need to give them the opportunity to experience success. Since when a teenager experiences success it increases their sense of mastery and competency so they feel good about themselves. Of course, I will add that these need to be true opportunities, so you can lend a helping hand but if you want to build a healthy sense of self-worth then the adolescent needs to figure out how to do some things on their own even if they're struggling.

It reminds me of one of my favourite psychology facts, I don't have a reference but a psychology lecturer mentioned it in an extremely dull lecture. She mentioned saying "you're so clever" to a baby is very harmful developmentally speaking instead you should say "you've worked so hard". The second saying starts teaching the child that you can overcome struggles with hard work, not innate intelligence.

<u>How To Improve Your Self-Worth?</u>

Building upon the last section as we move into our final section for this chapter, you're going to learn about how to increase your self-worth using five exercises.

Firstly, to improve your self-worth, you need to understand who you are because in essence, once you understand who you are, you can realise and decide for yourself that you are a worthy human being. As well as self-growth guru Adam Sicinski recommends asking yourself the following questions to help you increase your self-understanding:

Imagine that everything you have is suddenly taken away from you (i.e., possessions, relationships, friendships, status, job/ career, accomplishments and achievements, etc.);

Ask yourself the following questions:

a. What if everything I have was suddenly taken away from me?

b. What if all I had left was just myself?

c. How would that make me feel?

d. What would I actually have that would be of value?

Think about your answers to these questions and see if you can come to this conclusion: "No matter what happens externally and no matter what's taken away from me, I'm not affected internally";

Next, get to know yourself on a deeper level with

these questions:

a. Who I am? I am . . . I am not . . .

b. How am I?

c. How am I in the world?

d. How do others see me?

e. How do others speak about me?

f. What key life moments define who I am today?

g. What brings me the most passion, fulfilment, and joy?

Once you have a good understanding of who you are and what fulfils and satisfies you, it's time to look at what isn't so great or easy about being you. Ask yourself these questions:

a. Where do I struggle most?

b. Where do I need to improve?

c. What fears often hold me back?

d. What habitual emotions hurt me?

e. What mistakes do I tend to make?

f. Where do I tend to consistently let myself down?

Finally, take a moment to look at the flipside; ask yourself:

a. What abilities do I have?

b. What am I really good at?

How To Improve Your Self-Worth By Increasing Self-Acceptance?

Now that you have a better understanding of who you are, you can increase your self-worth by increasing your self-acceptance because you'll start to value yourself more once you forgive yourself for any areas that need to be improved, any struggles and bad habits that you have. For example, I needed to forgive myself constantly for my trauma responses during the worst of my mental health. I needed to forgive myself for always being tense, anxious and feeling like I was going to get raped again whenever I went into a new situation with new people and something I didn't control completely.

And since I've forgiven myself for my trauma responses I feel so much better about myself. Even now actually, I forgive myself for not knowing about relationships, not knowing about consensual sex and not knowing so many gay things that my friends take for granted. None of that is my fault and I forgive myself because my abuse was the reason I don't know these things. It is not my fault.

Therefore, to improve your self-acceptance, it is always useful to repeat the following statements:

"I accept the good, the bad and the ugly. I fully accept every part of myself including my flaws, behaviours, fears and qualities that I am not too proud of and this is how I am and I am at peace with that,"

I really like those statements and you might benefit from saying it once a day when you get up or you might benefit from saying it whenever you're struggling or doubting yourself. Just make sure you say it, accept it and internalise it. Then hopefully your mental health and your self-worth will improve over time.

How To Improve Self-Worth By Increasing Your Self-Love?

Now that you accept yourself for who you are, you can hopefully start to care as well as love yourself. In essence, this exercise is all about extending the kindness, love, compassion, tolerance and generosity that you hopefully show to others to yourself. For instance, start paying attention to your Self-talk, make sure it isn't too critical or overly harsh, and make sure that you aren't berating yourself at every chance you get. Make sure that you talk to yourself with positivity.

It's only in the past month or two that I've

become a lot better at this skill because I have had to. I have had to learn to be kind to myself because I hated myself so much, I just couldn't value or think of myself as being worthy because I always spoke so negatively about myself. That only harmed my mental health and actually made my struggles and difficulties even worse.

The following statements can help you if you need some support getting started:

"I feel valued and special. I love myself wholeheartedly. I am a worthy and capable person,"

Think about these statements and say them aloud and over time, you'll start to believe them and increase your self-love.

Improving Your Self-Worth By Recognising It

After you start to accept, understand and love yourself for who you are, you'll reach a point where you are no longer dependent on accomplishments, other people and other external factors for your self-worth. This is very healthy and that's why the best thing you can do for yourself and your own self-worth is to recognise all the great work that you've done. It is only because of you and all the work that *you* have put in that you've been able to accept, love and understand yourself for you.

That is a great achievement and I truly want you to be proud of yourself for that.

Therefore, as you continue to maintain your self-love, self-acceptance and self-worth, just remember to recognise how brilliant it is that you've achieved these things. As well as, it is always useful to remember the following:

- Your values come from inside yourself, from an internal measure that you have set for yourself.
- You no longer need to please other people to get self-worth.
- You have the power, no one else, to respond to circumstances and events based on your internal sources, your own resourcefulness and resources. These are the reflections of your true value to yourself and the world.
- Only you can control how you feel about yourself, regardless of what other people say, do or what happens around you.

Improve Your Self-Worth By Taking Responsibility For Yourself

The final exercise you can do to improve your self-worth is practice being responsible for yourself, your problems and your circumstances. In other words, this exercise focuses on being accountable for your actions. As a result, to take full responsibility, it's important that you do take responsibility for everything that happens to you whilst making sure you don't give your agency or personal power away to others. As well as you should acknowledge that you have the personal power to influence and change the circumstances and events of your life.

Personally, this is something that I realised when my anorexia was getting really bad and I was starting to get really sick. I had been putting off finding a counsellor for months and getting any actual mental health support for my anorexia, even though I had tried a few times. Yet as I started to get sicker because of malnutrition, I realised that I needed to take responsibility for my anorexia because no one was going to save me except myself. Anorexia was a massive problem in my life and I needed to save myself or my health would only get worse.

Now, I'm recovering nicely from my anorexia and I feel great about myself, but that recovery journey only started because I accepted responsibility for myself, my anorexia and my recovery.

Ultimately, these five exercises will help you to learn how to improve your self-worth and know that you have the power to change your life, for the better.

Conclusion

In the past two chapters, we have covered a lot of ground so I want to leave you with a message. After this chapter, we know that self-worth is a critical concept for both psychology researchers, students and psychologists and laypeople too. Since it is important for our mental health and relationships with both ourselves and others that we identify, build and maintain a normal and healthy sense of self-worth.

In essence, self-worth is all about learning how to become your authentic self so you can be happy, thrive and resilient in the face of challenges.

Normally, this is where I would give you questions to think about. Instead I would simply advise you to practice and do the questions and exercises that I've already included in this chapter. You'll learn a lot for sure and you'll be one step closer to knowing who you are.

WHY IS OUR SELF-IMAGE SO IMPORTANT?

When it comes to our mental health and our unshakable Self, our self-image and how we see ourselves is critical to making us feel good or bad about ourselves. If we imagine that we're a good person with a positive self-image then we feel great, if we have a negative self-image then this increases our risk of depression, anxiety and other negative mental health outcomes. Therefore, in this chapter, you'll learn what is our self-image, what are the effects of a positive and negative self-image and most importantly, how do we improve our self-image for our own mental health.

What Is Self-Image?

Our self-image is flat out critical in our social identity because it shapes how we engage with the world. As well as our self-image encompasses how we perceive ourselves psychologically, emotionally and our physical appearance. Also, our self-image includes how we view our expressions, our body and how we feel in our own skin has a large impact on our social interactions as well as sense of worth.

This is why trauma survivors can have a very negative self-image. I know after I was raped I felt disgusting and awful in my own skin and body so that coupled with my constant anxiety and other symptoms of Post-Traumatic Stress Disorder has extremely negative impacts on my social interactions and my sense of worth.

In addition, our self-image is connected to our self-perceptions and these influence almost every aspect of our life. For instance, our self-esteem, our relationships and more. When our self-image is negatively distorted, it negatively impacts our mental health and our social confidence. Since Dhawan & Kour (2024) found that people with negative self-image experienced reduced self-esteem, increased anxiety in social settings and they found it more difficult to make meaningful connections.

On the whole, it's important to learn about self-image so we can understand how it impacts our mental health. Then after we understand this aspect of the Self, we can take actionable steps towards strengthening our self-image and we can develop a more resilient self-image that empowers us towards being more confident and growing in all aspects of our lives.

Why Is Self-Image So Powerful?

The reason why our self-image is so powerful is that our self-perceptions play a massive role in our mental health and how we connect to other people. Since if you have a negative self-image then this can lead you to avoid social situations and feeling disconnected. Typically, this happens because you have a harsh inner critic then these self-image struggles impact aspects of your daily life and this highlights the importance of having a healthier relationship with your Self.

In my experience, during the worse of my mental health after my rape, when I seriously hated myself with all my might, it really made me feel unlovable, like a failure and like it was impossible for anyone to actually care about me. I talk about this more in *Healing As A Survivor* but when I found out my best friend and my other housemate were in a relationship, I had panic attacks for 18 hours straight and I collapsed three times. A lot of it wasn't about the relationship itself, it was largely because I truly believed no one could ever love me.

Trauma is a good personal example so you can see how me hating myself, and by extension having a negative self-image, played a massive role in maintaining and causing my mental health struggles.

Furthermore, Lopez and Polletta (2021) found there was a consistent link between mental health and self-image showing that a negative view of the Self can continue feelings of insecurity as well as impair someone's emotional resilience. Also, Liao et al. (2023) found people with negative self-image tended to process situations more negatively and this led to increases in emotional sensitivity and stress. Which believe me is not ideal.

Thankfully, there are ways to improve self-image through compassionate techniques so this improves a person's self-perceptions.

On the whole, this helps people to overcome their limiting beliefs, increase their chances of personal growth and improve their overall emotional well-being.

How Does Social Media Impact Self-Image?

Whilst I discuss this more in my book, *Social Media Psychology,* social media has increased people's need to have an idealised self-image. You only need to go on social media and see all the amazing and really successful things that your friends and family are doing. You can see all about the progress of their great relationship, their holidays and any job promotions. This tailored positivity increases the pressure on the people to maintain this idealised version of themselves and statistics from FHE Health suggest that 65% of men and 88% of women compare themselves to images on social media with the majority of people reporting that these comparisons harm their self-esteem.

Moreover, if you're constantly exposed to

this (fake) filtered and curated content then this increases your risk of developing a distorted self-perception, increasing your self-doubt and increasing your risk of depression and loneliness. Also, I would add from past podcast episodes that I have done that social media comparisons increase your risk of developing body image concerns and these can lead to eating disorders, body dysmorphia and muscle dysmorphia too.

Overall, it's important that people start to build a healthier relationship with social media so this includes setting boundaries and engaging in content that inspires self-acceptance and positivity in your life.

In the next chapter, you'll learn about how you can improve your self-image so you can continue to build your resilient, unshakable Self. Until then, here are some questions to get you thinking about what you've learnt in this chapter:

- How do you view yourself? Positively or negatively?
- Are there certain areas of your life that you have an overly negative self-image over?
- Do you think your use of social media helps or harms your self-image?

HOW CAN YOU IMPROVE YOUR SELF-IMAGE?

The last chapter allowed you to see that developing a negative self-image is not fun for your mental health and it isn't good for your sense of self. Since having a negative self-image makes you feel bad about your sense of self, so to use Tokito's quote again. A negative self-image means you cannot dig in with both feet and it doesn't allow all your doubts, hesitations and frustrations to disappear.

They will only increase and fuel them even more. This is not what we want when you're building your unshakable self and getting to know who you are.

Let's explore some ways how we can improve our self-image.

How Can Routines Help Improve Your Self-Image?

I've spoken before on The Psychology World Podcast about the importance of daily routines in protecting your mental health, like having a consistent sleep schedule. Yet another benefit of a consistent routine that you might build your structured daily habits or self-care practices is that they can help you to take control over your self-perceptions too. For instance, Kriakous et al. (2021) found that people who had daily self-care routines, like journaling, mindful breathing or meditation had a 20% decrease in perceived stress and a significant increase in emotional resilience within three weeks. As well as participants who maintained these consistent routines reported greater levels of self-compassion and self-efficacy. These are important factors for positive mental health and self-image.

In addition, even if you only have time (or only *think* you have time) for brief intentional habits then this can still benefit your self-image and mental health. Due to these habits activate regions in your brain like the prefrontal cortex, a brain region critical for emotional regulation and reward processing. This helps to improve your self-image over time because this approach helps an individual to improve their self-perception and this gradually improves their resilience and sense of personal empowerment.

Personally, I know that when I'm insanely busy doing other things other than the items on my To-Do list, my mental health starts to decrease, my perceived stress levels increase and I realise I need to be careful. I am a lot better than I used to be but I've actually just come back from a long day at university doing Ambassador work where I was Lead on a visit day for 17- and 18-year-olds so they could learn what happens at university and what university life is like. Then I went to a Postgraduate Talk on cultures so I haven't done a great amount of things today off my To-Do list. Right now I have a healthy level of stress because it is motivating me and I know how to handle these feelings of wanting to get a lot done within a short space of time.

Yet it goes to show how it is important to your mental health to have daily habits, routines and achieving what you want to get done.

<u>What Steps Can You Take To Improve Your Self-Image?</u>

Now we know why having a positive self-image is so important, let's look at some practical steps you could take to help develop a positive self-image. Of course, nothing in this book is ever any sort of official advice but there are a lot of useful tips.

Firstly, practice self-compassion. This has been one of the most powerful techniques that I have developed in my trauma healing and it has seriously improved my mental health over the past few months. I give a lot of information, techniques and support about self-compassion and how to do it in my book *Healing As A Survivor*. Therefore, instead of focusing on your perceived shortcomings and flaws, focus and move your inner dialogue to a dialogue of patience, self-love and self-acceptance. Something I do whenever a negative thought pops up is I twist it and make it more positive. For example, I have massive anxiety about mistakes in social relationships because of my past and some friendship trauma, so instead of thinking "I made a mistake so they're going to leave me and I've messed up the friendship" I tone it down to something like "I *might* have made a mistake and that's normal. Everyone makes mistakes because that is just what happens when interacting with other people and it probably isn't as bad as I fear,"

Self-compassion really helps you to increase your resilience because it nurtures your emotional health and this allows you to view yourself with more understanding and kindness.

Secondly, increase your social confidence over time, I have a lot more social confidence than I used to but I used to be really socially anxious. Even more so after my rape. Therefore, it's important if you want to develop a positive self-image to rebuild your social confidence over time by starting with small, manageable goals in social settings. For instance, you could attend a low-pressure gathering or practice taking photos of yourself in a safe space. Then over time as you gradually expose yourself to these situations, your comfort levels will increase and it will become easier to take part in larger social events as well as you will feel more confident being yourself and in your own skin.

As I recovered from my sexual trauma, and I only use this so I can give you a personal example even if you haven't been through trauma the example still stands. I would have mental health crises regardless of the social situation, whether they were big or small, and I would hate myself so much because I couldn't live and have a good life. As a result, over time, I exposed myself to small events and I gradually grew in confidence and now I am thriving thankfully. One example is that I joined the Dungeons and Dragons group that my best friend is in and I wouldn't leave their side and I would come home with them (we live together too) and I wouldn't go out with the others for dinner. Yet over time as I healed, I started going out with them for dinner and board games afterwards and it is amazing fun.

I feel a lot better about myself too.

Thirdly, as I mentioned earlier, develop a consistent, daily self-care ritual so you can prioritise your physical and mental health. This could include a morning meditation or run, keeping a gratitude diary or do mindful breathing exercises. These daily self-care habits are useful because they'll help you to centre your thoughts, increase your emotional stability and reinforce a positive view of your Self. It doesn't even need to be that long. These habits can only be five- or ten minutes if that is all the time you have.

Penultimately, and this is an important one, set some boundaries with yourself regarding social media. Since if you don't use social media with intent that allows you to cultivate a social media feed filled with positivity and authenticity then you will start feeling bad and develop a negative self-image. It isn't great to see lots of hot, muscular men or extremely thin women and your friends and family posting about their curated and filtered amazing lives. You will compare yourself to them and your self-image will take a hit. As a result, it's recommended that you follow accounts that inspire self-acceptance, personal growth and protect your mental health and you blocking or muting accounts that make you compare or feel bad.

Moreover, people recommend that you have designated times when you check social media and you don't scroll before bed, so you don't go to bed stressed. Also, not scrolling before bed helps to improve your sleep quality too. This all helps you to protect your mental health and your self-image.

Personally, I tend to avoid social media in general because it is filled with so much hate, misinformation and just rubbish. On Twitter, there are a few accounts I check in with at various points throughout the week and I avoid LinkedIn. For me, LinkedIn does negatively impact my mental health because everyone, including people I graduated with, post about their amazing jobs, their amazing research positions and how grateful they are to lecturers and universities they barely speak to. Most of LinkedIn is very fake as far as I'm concerned and it rarely talks about the struggles that people had to get to these positions.

Finally, and I was always going to include this one, if you are struggling with your self-image then please seek support from a mental health professional. It might be useful for you to work with a therapist or mental health professional who can provide you with tailored support as well as strategies to improve your self-image. A therapist can help you identify how to navigate difficult emotions, unhelpful thought processes and develop a structured plan for self-acceptance. This could be through therapy, mindfulness training or another way but expert guidance helps you to become empowered by holistically addressing your self-image challenges.

Conclusion

At the end of these two chapters focused on self-image, you know that your self-image plays a major role in your mental health because it impacts confidence, resilience and how comfortable you feel in your own body and social situations. Thankfully, your self-image isn't fixed so there are ways to cultivate a positive self-image so your mental health can improve too. You can improve your self-image by practising self-care on a daily basis, setting boundaries with social media, talking to a therapist and more.

Ultimately and from personal experience, if you have a negative self-image, especially a self-image that makes you hate yourself because you're a failure, you're pathetic, you're worthless. Embracing self-compassion, practising relaxation and other techniques that promote resilience and self-acceptance is honestly one of the most beneficial things that you can do to your mental health.

As a result, my questions for you at the end of this chapter are the following:

- How do you view yourself?
- How might you improve your self-image?
- What boundaries could you set on your social media use?
- What daily self-care routines do you have?

HOW DO YOU BUILD RESILIENCE AND THE SELF?

When it comes to the different facets of your behaviour that can contribute to having an Unshakable Self, resilience is a key factor. Due to everyone needs psychological resilience because it is being resilient that allows us to effectively pick ourselves up after something goes wrong. As well as resilience refers to our ability to quickly recover from a difficulty so this can refer to something going wrong at work, us not getting a certain grade at school or university or resilience can refer to trauma. Since after witnessing or experiencing a traumatic or difficult event, be it sexual violence, physical violence or more, resilience can help us with our recovery from the trauma.

Therefore, in this chapter, you'll learn about how to build resilience so you can use it in your everyday life and if you ever experience trauma, your resilience can help you with your recovery.

Why Do We Need To Talk About Resilience?

Back in the early days of my podcast, I did the podcast episodes called *3 Tips To Build Psychological Resilience* and *3 New Tips To Build Psychological Resilience*. As you can see, I was very creative with my episode names back in 2020 and 2021, yet as I preluded to in the introduction, experiencing trauma and surviving traumatic events can be very physically, emotionally and psychologically difficult for people and the amount of resilience a person had was an important factor in their ability to deal with the trauma.

Now before we continue I want to jump in here and add two very important pieces of information. Firstly, I can only speak for sexual trauma in the context of this chapter but you can still be an extremely resilient person like me and seriously struggle with the aftermath of your sexual assault. If you're struggling, it doesn't mean that you're not resilient and all those disgusting myths that exist around being a "victim". Experiencing sexual trauma can shatter your resilience.

Also, resilience can be learnt so if you aren't a very resilient person or you're a trauma survivor who feels like they have no resilience (even though you probably have more resilience than you realise. That's a lesson I need to keep teaching myself) then that's okay because you can learn to be more resilient over time.

In addition, the content for this chapter largely comes from Roeckner et al. (2021) who concluded that individual differences in threat cue processing are related to the person's resilience whilst their higher-order executive functioning is less consistent and their relationship with resilience changes over time. In other words, both resilience and higher-order executive functioning are both stable factors in predicting how your brain responds to threats that will impact the likelihood of your resilience and how it changes over time.

Also, the researchers found that whilst trauma is very common, even people who experience trauma most often can recover over time. Their resilience is a major protective factor during the aftermath of their trauma so it's important to help grow people's resilience.

That's why we're going to look at five different ways to help people grow their resilience so we help people recover following trauma.

How To Build Resilience?

Let Yourself Carefully Think About The Traumatic Experience

Now I say carefully because I have tried, and I'm sure a lot of other people have to, to think about the traumatic experience in great depth without much care. This was a massive mistake for me personally and I always end up getting a lot more distressed after the fact, because it wasn't careful.

Therefore, carefully thinking about a traumatic event can be useful because it allows you to think about the trauma in the context of the event. As well as you don't need to come to any conclusions about why this happened to you, and instead be thinking carefully about the trauma, you're preventing your brain from overgeneralising. In other words, you're stopping your brain from taking the trauma and applying it to other parts of your life. This is a massive problem that I used to have when I was writing this chapter, because whenever I see a very overweight man, I get extremely distressed because it reminds me of my attacker.

This is an unfortunate example of how my brain has overgeneralised my sexual assault to other areas of my life so much so that even going out in public can be a minefield of distress for me. I still go out and live my life but there is a lot of distress and anxiety that accompanies me.

Overall, carefully thinking about the traumatic experience can be helpful for processing the emotions associated with the experience and over time the intensity of the experiences and all the negative, distressing emotions it evokes should decrease.

Let Yourself Engage In Positive Self-Care

Whenever you experience a traumatic event, you still need to look after yourself and I'm smiling as I write this because I seriously did not do this at certain times in the last 17 weeks. I remember back in very early July because me moving in with my best friend was so distressing, so triggering and so bad for me. My eating disorder had activated so badly and my best friend was really worried for me, and I basically did everything against self-care. Thankfully I am fine now in that department and me and my best friend really enjoy living together, but after trauma and when you face triggers, it can be very easy not to look after yourself.

Please try to remember to look after yourself.

You are the most important person and you need to look after yourself.

Therefore, you need to eat healthy foods, stay active, get good sleep (I would flat out love that at the moment) because all these are important supporters of your resilience. Due to doing all these self-care things helps our brains to work better and our anxiety and mood improves when we're rested and well-fed.

Please take care of your mind and body.

<u>Allow Yourself To Reach Out To Trusted People For Support</u>

Let's face it, because The Psychology World Podcast is a clinical psychology podcast in all but name and I am an aspiring clinical psychologist so I will always bring up this point. You cannot deal with trauma alone, you seriously can't so please reach out to other people for support.

When it comes to support after a traumatic experience, this can take different forms depending on the other person and the level of your relationship with them. For example, you might just want to hang out with a friend that you have a positive connection with because you enjoy spending time with them. Actually, a relatively new friend just Whatsapped whilst I was writing this chapter saying he wants to come round tomorrow. This new friend isn't a person I could ever have rape conversations with but I really like spending time with him and I find that really relaxing and it gives me a few hours away from all the distress and rape stuff coming on in my head.

That is one option for you.

Equally, on the other side of the spectrum of friendships, you can talk to friends and family members that you have a close relationship with for specific support. For instance, whilst my best friend is currently 181 miles away (we joked about the distance, it isn't weird I know the exact distance from where I live to the town their parents live in), they were still very firm with me about contacting them if I need anything or need any contact. And over the past week, we've had some in-depth supportive conversations but mostly, it's been a case of them letting me talk or send them long, distressed messages because that's what I need.

I sent them one yesterday where I literally had to write down what I was going to do next because something that happens in rape survivors is they sometimes cannot make any decisions. That popped up for me yesterday, so my hack around that is after making sure I actually can't make decisions (it's always the case) I text my best friend and I talk myself through it.

In other words, get support however you need it and have open and honest conversations with your friends and loved ones about what they need from you.

Ultimately, getting this support will help to improve your mood and this increases your resilience. As well as if you share your experience with them then this can be even more helpful. It is very healing to say things out loud to another person who wants to be there for you and support you.

Let Yourself Consider Your Core Values and How To Connect With These During Distressing Times

This is advice I have seen time and time again and it is still something I really struggle with.

There are a lot of different ways you can do this, but the entire point of this tip is to help you do what matters to you, brings you joy and improves your mental health. For example, it's important that you take a few minutes to decide what matters most to you. Such as, it could be your community, connecting with your friends or family, your religious or spiritual practices or a hobby. For me, what matters most is my writing, being a good friend, my business, psychology, my podcast helping people and so on.

As a result, I've been trying to focus on my fiction and nonfiction writing as much as possible during the past 17 weeks. It has been flat out impossible but I am happier in this great month of August 2024 because I am able to dedicate so much time to my fiction and nonfiction projects. I am still having to balance my writing with business stuff and me working on my academic paper, but I still really enjoy those aspects of my life too.

And it helps me manage all the distress, negative mental health and sheer crippling Post-Traumatic Stress symptoms that paralyse me on a weekly or daily basis. Doing what I enjoy just helps me realise how good my life is when I'm not experiencing these hellish mental health outcomes.

Okay, maybe I have been doing this tip more than I thought.

In terms of yourself, you might want to do something really basic to help you engage in your core values. You might read a book, watch films with a friend or loved one or go out to specific places that you enjoy. Like a museum, a park or a woodland.

On the whole, this helps to increase your resilience because you are doing what matters most to you and when we all live a life that is consistent with our values, then our mood increases, our mental health improves and we're happy.

You Need To Avoid Unhelpful Patterns Of Substance And/ or Alcohol Abuse

When I was putting this chapter together, I was very, very careful to make sure the subheadings didn't sound like I was ordering you to do anything. I made an exception for this one because I've seen and I've read a lot of very heartbreaking literature on the consequences of substance and alcohol abuse on survivors and I don't want that for you.

Since for a lot of people who have survived trauma or distress, they really want to push away these feelings by numbing their emotions with substances or alcohol. This works for a time but the problem tends to get worse and grow over time and this leads to a wide range of mental and physical health complications later on. A very bad liver is one that springs to mind.

As a result, it's important that you're

mindful about alcohol and substance use if you've been through a difficult and traumatic situation because this helps to reduce the chance of unhelpful responses developing as a coping mechanism.

And I'm not going to sit here and say that this is easy. Back when I was having my mental breakdown in August 2023 because of my insanely homophobic and dysfunctional social environment and all the decade-long trauma and abuse that led to, I was so tempted to try and find some drugs. I was seriously considering trying substance abuse because I just wanted the pain to stop, but I didn't. Since I knew substance abuse wasn't helpful, it wasn't healthy and it would only damage me even more in the long term.

I did therapy instead and it helped me more than I could ever express.

Conclusion

Ultimately, resilience is a critical skill for life because it enables us to pick ourselves up after we've experienced a negative life event. Yet resilience isn't a given for everyone and if you've been through trauma then your resilience can be shattered. The latter is what I've found after my sexual assault.

Thankfully, resilience can be improved, practiced and you can become more resilient over time as you put in the time and effort to improve this trait. The key to building resilience is knowing it will take some time, this won't be something that happens overnight and if you rush it, you will be frustrated and you might risk quitting. So please, be kind to yourself, reach out for support when you need it and remember, there is life after trauma.

Your trauma doesn't have to define, control or ruin your life. You can heal and recover, and resilience is just one part of that great journey.

WHY ARE MORE AUTHENTIC PEOPLE HAPPIER?

As a podcast host, there is something very fun about going through the archives of The Psychology World Podcast, and by that I mean seeing how much the podcast has evolved over the years. This next chapter comes from the very early days of the podcast because the actual content is only 500-words long.

However, I want to include it in this book because a lot of what we're talking about with the Unshakable Self is the importance of being authentic. You can only be authentic if you know who you are, what your values are and everything else about *you* instead of what society, others and the world tell you, you are.

As a result, back in 2014, psychology researchers at Louisiana Tech University published a very important study using data collected from college students about their level of authenticity as well as their life satisfaction. Overall, their results demonstrated that the more authentically people lived their lives, the happier they were with their life.

Additionally, as a human branding and social psychology person this is perfect for you as this builds into the idea of human branding where you need to connect with people and get them to know, like and trust you.

Interestingly, the study found that there were three reasons for these research findings.

Reason Number One:

Firstly, the more authentic you are, the more likely you are to live your own life as well as follow your own path in live. Due to the fact that you will most probably do what feels most natural to you so you will develop your interests as well as develop your curiosity for that interest. Overall, making you more likely to become high skilled and an expert in that chosen skill.

Personally, as I'm really interested in human branding and I live authentically. I actively develop and learn about social psychology and things related to human branding so I can become better and more skilled at human branding.

Reason Number Two:

Secondly, the more authentic you are, the more you should be able to resistant outside pressure from people around you who want you to be a different version of yourself or at least do another job. Yet being authentic results in you being free to be yourself and follow what you want to do.

The Final Reason:

Finally, and my personal favourite as a massive human branding fan; is being authentic allows you to have more meaningful relationships with people. As well as authenticity makes you less willing to spend your valuable time with people who don't care about you.

Personally, I completely agree with this final reason because being authentic is all about being true to yourself so you shouldn't have to deal with people who don't like nor care about yourself.

Conclusion:

In conclusion, people who are more authentic tend to be happier in their lives because they tend to follow their own paths in life, they can resistant outside pressure and be themselves as well as they tend to have more deeper and meaningful relationships with people.

HOW DOES SENSE OF SELF CONNECT TO DEPRESSION?

In a previous chapter, we learnt a lot about the social psychological theories behind the Self and we learnt a few different facts about how these theories impact our mental health. However, in this chapter, I want to explore the impact of the Self on our mental health in a lot more depth, so we can see another reason why the Self is important to us. Therefore, in this chapter, you'll learn how does our sense of self connect to depression, how can self-discrepancy theory explain depression and more.

Why Should People With Depression Pay Attention To Sense of Self?

Whenever people experience depression, we always tend to focus on our symptoms. For example, when I was severely depressed for a few months during the worse of my mental health after my rape. All I could focus on was how depressed I was, how hard it was to do even the smallest things, how I didn't have the motivation to do anything and so on. It was the symptoms that I focused on.

However, Kopala-Sibley and Zuroff (2019) highlighted that what we should actually be focusing on isn't our symptoms. Instead, we should be focusing on our sense of Self and the researchers pointed to Self-Discrepancy theory as a good explanation of this recommendation. Since the theory was created by psychology professor Edward Higgins and he proposed that the Self has three aspects. These are our actual Self, our Ideal Self and the Ought Self.

Firstly, the actual Self is who we think we are and this is related to how we assess our characteristics. For example, how we assess our looks, our intelligence as well as our talent. For me, I assess myself to be terribly untalented at winning board games but as me and my friends say, at the game of life, I'll hopefully always be better than them.

Secondly, the Ought Self is related to what you or other people think you should be. For instance, if you think you should be better at maths, English or another subject entirely. Or if you believe you should be smart enough to be a doctor and you are not that is a small example of a discrepancy between the Actual and Ought Self.

Thirdly, the Ideal Self is related to what you wish you could or would be. Also, Strauman and Higgins (1987) found that people are likely to get depressed when there is a mismatch between their actual and ideal Self. I agree with this finding because the main reasons why I got so depressed after my rape was I wanted to and I felt like I should have been able to go out, live my life, be social and enjoy my summer like everyone else was (my Ideal Self), but I couldn't. My PTSD was too bad, my anxiety was too severe and I was having way too many panic attacks to even remotely go out by myself (my actual Self). Hence, I got depressed because I felt so down, lonely and isolated because of it.

Another example is that if you believe that you're smart and hard-working but in reality, your work situation limits your progress. Then this causes your "actual" Self to become a lower-achieving version of your ideal self. Possibly leading to depression. A more specific example is that if you believe you have the experience, skills and expertise to be able to become a fully qualified clinical psychologist but you can never seem to be able to get onto the doctorate. Then this will start to cause a mismatch, leading to possible depression.

As a result, Strauman and Higgins (1988) suggests when you are depressed, it is important to address this mismatch between the actual and ideal Self. As well as a recent meta-analysis by Mason et al. (2019) confirms that it is important in treating depression to decrease their mismatch.

This is even more important when we consider that how much of a match there is between the actual and ideal Self determines our self-esteem too (Moretti and Higgins, 1990). Self-esteem is another factor in the development as well as maintenance of depression (Hilbert et al., 2019).

Building upon this, people with low self-esteem also have less grey matter in the regions of their brain in charge of adapting to stress as well as feeling pride. Also, these people have less grey matter in the brain regions in charge of "theory of mind", regions that help us to infer what other people are thinking. Overall, self-esteem is a big influence on the development and maintenance of depression.

How Can Self-Discrepancy Theory Help Combat Depression?

We can use self-discrepancy theory to help us combat depression because we can start to change our internal narrative. These are the stories we have in our head about ourselves and how other people perceive us, because how we perceive our Self determines our actual Self and this leads to our Ideal Self. To start changing our internal narratives, we need to think about how our depressed assumptions impact us and then we need to change them based on what we know from psychological research.

For instance, if I was doing this last year after my rape, I would focus on how my trauma makes me feel like I couldn't go outside, I couldn't be social, I couldn't do anything and I was just a failure of a human being. Yet I know none of that is true and I was always being too hard on myself and not always giving myself the time to grieve and heal that I deserved.

Here are some ways how these internal narratives can be changed, but as always nothing in this book is ever any sort of official advice. And please, talk to a mental health professional if you are experiencing negative mental health outcomes and depression.

Firstly, you can change your internal narratives by using positive self-talk because when you're depressed, you believe that the mismatch between your Ideal and Actual Self is fixed so you are doomed. However, you need to change this self-talk to become more positive and truthful to be honest. You need to focus on how your brain can change throughout its lifetime and you can always learn new things regardless of your age.

Secondly, you can change by using self-promotion instead of prevention strategies, because when you're depressed you might be harsher to yourself. This is why self-compassion is so important and self-compassion is a proven route to help you achieve your goals. As well as it isn't false self-praise either because you are smart enough to know when this praise feels fake. Instead, it is simply about providing the supportive emotional environment that you need to be able to reach your goals. Hence, why it's a good idea to focus on promotion instead of prevention, so you focus on what you need to do instead of what you need to prevent.

I know from personal experience that once I started to focus more on self-compassion and how I needed to live my life instead of being fearful that all my distressing trauma responses would activate. I started to feel a lot happier because yes, bad things would happen. I would get distressed but I would be okay and I saw these incidents as ways to learn and heal, so I wouldn't get as triggered in the future.

Finally, you can switch to internal guides because when you're depressed you might feel like it is impossible to get closer to your ideal Self. When this happens, you should switch your attention from looking outside to looking inside because depression by its very nature will block out your ability to see opportunities from the outside. This is why you should try to switch to your internal self-guides. The first guide is a sense of possibility where you can imagine what you want. Then instead of thinking about what you want as being in the future, consider it done now. Simulate this want towards your goal and afterwards you can focus on what you need to change to make this goal a reality.

<u>Conclusion</u>

I know we've focused on depression a lot over the years, but it is always useful and interesting to look at depression from a new angle. It was great to see depression from a social psychology and applied perspective in this chapter. Since it got us thinking about how the mismatch between the actual and ideal Self can be a developing and maintaining factor in depression. Then it is only by decreasing this mismatch that someone can hope to start taking steps towards their healing.

My questions at the end of this chapter are:

- Think about your actual self, how do you see yourself and your characteristics?
- Think about your ideal self, what do you wish you could and would be?
- Is there a discrepancy?
- If so, how big? And how does this impact your mental health?

WHAT IS EMOTIONAL DEPENDENCY AND LOCUS OF EVALUATION?

I wanted to include this chapter in the book because it sets up the groundwork for our next chapter. Since after a person has experienced trauma and if they were unloved as a child then they might develop Emotional Dependency or an External Locus of Evaluation in order to fill a hole felt inside them that has left them feeling empty, alone and unloved. In this chapter, you'll learn what is emotional dependency, why it is so damaging to our relationships and our mental health. As well as this chapter connects to the Self, because this psychological concept draws a lot on the different parts of the Self, our self-esteem and what kind of relationship we have with our self.

It is a fascinating topic, so let's dive into it.

What Is Emotional Dependency?

What I'll do is that I'll explain how normal healthy relationships work so you can understand emotional dependency is unhealthy. Then I'll give you some good definitions including my own personal way because some of the definitions get a little hard to grasp.

Therefore, we all know that emotional *support* in relationships is normal, healthy and it is seriously needed. Since we all like to know that our boyfriend, girlfriend, whatever is there for us after a bad day at work and they are able to support us. That is perfectly normal and it is expected and needed in social relationships.

We all need in relationships with our romantic partners and friendships to be able to support each other. Also we cannot have great relationships without a good level of healthy personal intimacy where we feel safe to disclose things about ourselves.

That is all healthy and normal.

In addition, emotional support helps us to feel good about ourselves, it increases self-esteem and our confidence.

However, when someone becomes emotionally *dependent* on another person then this can make a relationship unhealthy and rather toxic. Due to if a person is dependent on someone else then they cannot function very well or self-soothe effectively. This means that we need to rely significantly on other people to provide this for us and this typically comes in the form of assuring we are good enough and we deserve their unconditional love.

As a result, when we talk about romantic relationships, this leads us to be very unsure and concerned about our partner's commitment and/ or approval towards us. This makes us focus on our own doubts about the relationships and our self-doubts. Leading people to feel insufficient in the relationship and our love (or friendship love) is overtaken by our fear. People with emotional dependency typically have concerns about will they abandon me, replace me and leave me? Ultimately the person with emotional dependence becomes reliant on the reassurance of the other person to feel valued, safe and secure.

Leading to relationship degradation.

The main reason for this is simply because it is hard to love someone whilst letting that person be whoever they want to be when we are trying to cover up our own insecurities. With these insecurities typically generated in earlier life experiences and childhood, because when our parents weren't able to make us securely attach to them, this harms us.

How Do I Describe Emotional Dependency?

Because emotional dependency deeply explores childhood attachment styles and whatnot, I want to quickly summarise all of it so we can move on to some other sections.

Therefore, I describe emotional dependency as when people don't love a child, or they didn't love a particular part of them enough as a child. This leaves a massive hole in that child that they desperately want to fill with some kind of love, safety and security. This leads to them in later life forming unhealthy attachments with friends, romantic partners and others in order to fulfil that hole inside them and the person wants someone to offer them the unconditional love, security and safety they were never given as a child.

For example, the sexuality part of my Self was never loved as a child and it was deeply traumatised and abused. This left me really wanting someone, anyone to give the sexuality part of my Self a feeling of safety, security and a kind of love (more like validation these days). So that's why whenever I form a close relationship (which I rarely do these days because of autism and past trauma) I do tend to make it toxic in relatively short order. Simply because I want, I need that sense of love, safety and security that I was never ever given as a child.

Now I will point out here that all the other parts of my Self were given extreme amounts of love, safety and security. Therefore, people can develop a more general kind of emotional dependency or they can form a narrow type like I have.

Or should I say *had*, past tense.

In addition, people who develop emotional dependency end up finding it next to impossible to internalise the validation and assurance that someone gives them. Meaning they need to keep hearing it again and again and they find it hard to make it part of their self-image, and fully integrate that part of the Self into their overall Self.

How Does Emotional Dependency Destroy Relationships?

Then to hammer this point out before we move onto the "cures" or therapy techniques for emotional dependency, emotional dependency typical breaks relationships because the emotionally dependent person wears down the other person with their constant or common requests for reassurance that they're cared about, loved and that their partner wants to spend time with them. The problem with this is that giving in to these requests doesn't erase all the pain, suffering and it doesn't fill the hole inside the person.

It really doesn't.

Therefore, as these requests continue over

time, it wears down the other person until they reach a breaking point.

Now I will admit that the people who have to spend with emotionally dependent people are flat out amazing. They do actually go through so much out of "love" (if they're in a romantic relationship) or dedication to the friendship and that causes them their own pain and annoyance. They are flat out amazing and great people who putting up with it and trying their hardness to help the emotionally dependent person.

But they do reach a breaking point and I seriously don't blame them. This is hard on everyone and these friends and romantic partners are heroes and incredible for just trying to last as long as they can.

Yet ultimately this is down to the emotionally dependent person to fix and get some kind of psychological support so they don't have to be emotionally dependent anymore.

Overall, emotional dependency leaves a person not *wanting* but *needing* reassurance desperately so they can help reduce some of the pain, suffering and uncertainty inside them. They just want someone to help fill the hole into themselves that just needs love, security and safety.

But this isn't healthy and this has to change.

How Can Emotional Dependency Be Cured?

I have to admit that nothing in psychology can be "cured" but emotional dependency are psychological wounds on a person. Therefore, they can be healed over time with enough information, dedication and motivation so the emotionally dependent person can work through their trauma and past and learn how to improve their lives.

Since as my therapist put it, at the end of the day, a partner, a friend, whoever can give me as much validation, as much safety and as much security as I want. Yet I know it will never be enough because basically as soon as I leave them I started feeling unsafe, in danger and uncertain again. It was simply how my mind used to work and I knew that wasn't healthy, but I didn't know how to change it.

That's why people who are emotionally dependent on others need to learn how to independently cope and ultimately provide themselves with a sense of security, safety and love.

Which I have to admit we are in an extremely powerful position to do that nowadays because we aren't children anymore. We are adults, we have the knowledge, we have the words and we hopefully have the life situations that allow us to provide ourselves with these three senses now.

In addition, there is a fair amount of information and resources online to help us overcome our emotional dependency. Including something called "Reparenting" ourselves or Transactional Analysis, which my therapist mentioned in passing and I must do a podcast episode on at some point because I know that will make me look it up.

Furthermore, here are some other tips I found online about overcoming emotional dependency and I think these are all really helpful. Then we'll move onto the extremely powerful technique of Locus of Evaluations because this is what allowed me to basically kill my Emotional Dependency issues.

- Deal with your past trauma

- Heal with emotions and your emotional wounds
- Understand your triggers
- Increase your circle of friends
- internalise locus of evaluation
- Distance from yourself from the relationship (think of this as a behavioural experiment because you'll see you won't die by being separated from the relationship)
- Do your own interests away from the relationship
- Ask what does your friend or partner need from you in the relationship (this is more aimed at partners to be honest)
- Know you are as good as the person you're emotionally dependent on
- Reparenting and know the areas you need to reparent yourself in
- Understand you have the right to talk about your positive and negative feelings even if it risks upsetting others (within reason of course. Don't be a horrible person for the sake of it)

What Is The Locus of Evaluation?

As proposed by Feltham and Dryden (1993), a person's Locus of Evaluation is the place from which a person makes their judgements about themselves, the others and the world, with the term first being used by Carl Rogers.

Therefore, a person can operate from an internal or external locus of evaluation. If a person uses an internal locus of evaluation then they trust themselves, they get their positive and negative evaluations from inside them and they get their sense of self-worth from themselves.

Nonetheless, if a person operates from an external locus of evaluation then this means they get their sense of self-worth, self-esteem and they internalise the value judgements about themselves from important others. This is normally because of childhood conditions.

In addition, it is important to note here that these are never the same for two people or even two aspects of the self. Since whenever it comes to me being a psychology student, a writer, a podcast and basically every single part of my Self (except until recently sexuality) I operated from a place of internal Locus of Evaluation. Due to I know that whenever I write something (be it nonfiction, fiction or university-related) I do the best I can do in that moment in time and I will improve over time.

Therefore, whatever other people think doesn't make me devalue myself and I don't get my sense of self-worth from other people. At least 99% of the time, I always love to hear from you podcast listeners but some bad comments won't make me want to shut the podcast because I believe I'm useless.

However, when it comes to the Sexuality Part of me because that was never loved, given safety or anything as a child. That part of my Self was left behind as the other aspects of the Self developed in healthy, normal ways so I had to change my Locus of Evaluation and bring it.

I did this mainly through a lot of memoir-ish writing and just reflecting and learning about reparenting and Locus of Evaluations. And over time I just realised I really don't care what other people think of sexuality and how I am and what I do with my life. It is honestly a tiny part of my life but because it was so abused and traumatised it has caused me massive problems in my life.

But now I simply no longer care about the

value judgements. I also accepted some harsh truths about my life and my personal situation that helped me to bring in my Locus of Evaluation too. Since I know, truly know that only I can make myself feel safe, loved and secure and I did some reality checks too because some traumas from my childhood just don't apply these days.

Finally, a good thing to realise when you're working through emotional dependency is to realise that you don't *need* anyone (including the person you're emotionally dependent on) to give you safety, love and security because only you can give yourself that sense. But you can *want* them to still be in your life.

There is a massive difference there. *Need* is about you not being able to function without them and *want* is you just wanting them to be there as a friend, a lover but ultimately you can function fine without them. Since you gave yourself that power back.

Conclusion

Overall, emotional dependency is about when a child isn't given love, security and safety they will find other unhealthy ways to have it in the future. They might seek constant reassurance, love and safety from a friend or a romantic partner. Yet over time this constant reassurance does wear a relationship down, normally to breaking point.

Thankfully, there are ways to overcome emotional dependency including psychological therapy, reparenting and readjusting your Locus of Evaluation.

Personally, by the time this podcast episode goes out I would have had three weeks (4 sessions) of therapy and honestly it has been the best money I have ever met. Due to I know how to have healthy relationships now, I know how to trust myself and give myself everything I never had as a child and I know moving forward that will be extremely important.

And honestly, I look back at my mental health breakdown the week before I started therapy and the week I started it, and I don't know how that person is anymore. I know that scared, traumatised and abused part of my Self is still there but he has no power over me now. He will not control my life, he will not make decisions because he's healed. Or he is healing and now I am learning how to live life with my a decade's worth of trauma, pain and suffering inside me.

Granted I'll admit I have no idea who I am in regards to my Sexuality Self because since it was first developed inside me, it isn't filled with pain, suffering and self-torture. It is free so I am definitely looking forward to exploring that part of me in the future and seeing how all these different parts of my Self interact.

I know therapy can be a scary time and thing to do, but if you need it, definitely do it because it has the power to change your life for the better.

HOW CAN YOU HEAL FROM FAMILY TRAUMA BY SETTING BOUNDARIES?

As I've mentioned in a past chapter, a large part of having a resilient, empowered self relies on you being able to set and reinforce boundaries. From personal experience, I know this is very hard for people who have been through trauma, especially when it comes to family trauma. Therefore, the next two chapters are going to focused on helping you develop the skills needed to set and reinforce this difficult type of boundary. As a result, your boundaries and your actions will be more in-line with your values, wants and desires and in face of difficult family members, you'll be a little more unshakable.

This chapter came about because I needed to start learning how to deal with family trauma a lot more after my rape, but I have never been able to do this I started my rape healing, so the next two chapters are the result of my research and my efforts to thankfully try and build better relationships with my family.

Since when it comes to healing from family trauma, it's flat out critical to learn how to set effective boundaries. These boundaries allow you to heal, protect yourself and build healthier relationships with family members that might have treated you badly before. Their bad or inappropriate treatment doesn't always have to be intentional or malicious, but it can be. My abuse wasn't intentionally malicious but it had done a lot of psychological damage to me over the past decade. As well as was massively amplified by my rape, and even if you haven't been through additional trauma as you try and heal from the damaging impact of dysfunctional families, setting boundaries is beyond critical. Therefore, in this clinical psychology podcast episode, you'll learn why setting boundaries is important with family members, how to do it and now. If you enjoy learning about trauma healing, distributional families and now then this is a great episode for you.

How Does Setting Boundaries Help Heal Family Trauma?

The reason why setting boundaries helps clients to help from family trauma is because by setting boundaries, you're helping yourself and other people to understand what is and what is not okay in your relationship. As well as with you being an adult child, it means you have a lot of freedom to set boundaries and limits with your family that will help you to improve your relationships over time. For example, you could set a limit on how much time and energy you invest with them. Also, you setting boundaries might involve invoking your right to self-care and personal autonomy and this is perfectly okay even if it does mean creating a certain distance from particular family members.

Additionally, by setting boundaries, you aren't saying that you don't love your family. Instead setting boundaries means that you are trying to stay connected as well as have a healthy, mature relationship with your family.

Of course, it is worth noting that unfortunately some people just aren't able to have healthy relationships so you may need to distance yourself from them.

Moreover, it's important to know that your boundaries act as a protective shield around you so you are less likely to be hurt by the dysfunctional, immature relationship that your family trauma has caused. Ultimately, setting boundaries with family members helps to protect yourself against further harm and they allow you to reclaim a sense of agency over your life.

And because this is a topic that I struggle a lot with, I want to stress here that asserting your own needs might be incredibly scary but it is so important. Asserting your needs helps you to break free from the patterns of dysfunction as well as co-dependency that effectively made up your upbringing.

I talk about this struggle more in my

Work-In-Progress book that focuses on my rape counselling. When I first had the conversation with my Mum about what I needed, the struggles I was facing and everything I was dealing with. I was shaking, terrified and I felt sick, but it worked out okay and everything has improved in the past week. Of course, there will always be challenges ahead but it is progress and it is the small victories you need to celebrate.

How Else Can Boundaries Help Trauma Healing?

Some other ways how setting boundaries can help clients heal from family trauma includes reduced stress. Setting boundaries helps to reduce stress because let's face it, toxic family interactions are extremely draining so boundaries help you to manage the level of stress that these interactions create and you can limit your exposure to these interactions. Therefore, you can focus on your health and wellbeing instead of focusing on the fallout and draining nature of these toxic interactions.

Secondly, setting boundaries can help your sense of safety because boundaries give you a safe space to heal. Since my limiting contact with toxic family members as well as friends and any other toxic people in your life, you can minimise any further emotional harm. I definitely agree with this point because as bad as my mental health is at the time of writing, setting boundaries and expectations with my family has given me one less concern or stressor in my life. This means I can focus, heal and think about other things instead of negative interactions, and I'm already seeing how my interactions with my family are becoming a lot more positive and better for my mental health.

Thirdly, setting boundaries can help to reduce your triggers because toxic family members tend to engage in behaviours that trigger your negative memories or negative emotions. As a result, boundaries help to minimise your exposure to these triggers so you can process your past trauma in a safe and controlled environment. And this is a great point because there have been times when my family have seriously triggered me because of my sexual trauma with some comments, a non-consensual touch or hug and some invalidation. Yet because I set boundaries, I have to deal with these triggers less and that has had a good impact on my mental health.

In addition, self-care is a great benefit of setting boundaries, because boundaries help you to focus on your own mental health and wellbeing. As well as boundaries allow you to treat yourself with the respect and kindness you deserve and this is a critical part of healing from trauma. Something I am needing to get better at. Also, boundaries can free up your time, energy and even money so you can partake in healing activities.

Building upon the last point, setting boundaries helps you to improve your self-esteem because boundaries help you to communicate and truly *feel* your self-worth. Because I know firsthand how people not respecting your boundaries, your consent and your self-worth makes you feel useless, awful and like dirt. Yet you are worth so much, you are clever, brilliant and a great person who deserves so much more. Therefore, by communicating your healthy boundaries, you are showing that you deserve to be treated respectfully by others and you will never tolerate being mistreated ever again.

This reminds me to mention that you need to reinforce your boundaries too, but that's something we mention again later.

Finally, setting boundaries helps you to break the cycle of dysfunction in your life. Since dysfunctional family dynamics and patterns of behaviour are often passed down you're the generations so setting boundaries helps to disrupt this cycle. Thus, you can build healthier relationships that focus on respect and genuine connection instead of these maladaptive dysfunctional patterns of behaviour.

As well as it's useful to note that every time you stand up for yourself by focusing on your own health and wellbeing, you are becoming a powerful example for future generations. Due to you are truly showing it is possible to overcome these dysfunctional family patterns of behaviour.

<u>How To Deal With Resistant Family Members?</u>

As much as I wish I could tell you that all your family members will be perfectly happy with you setting boundaries, I cannot. There will be a few or maybe the majority of toxic family members and loved ones that think you are being outrageous, unfair and evil for wanting to set boundaries. For example, my family was annoyed at me and very defensive at first when it came to me setting boundaries because everything was my fault.

Furthermore, the strategies that your toxic family members use on you, like guilt, will make you enforcing your boundaries even more difficult. Since you'll be dealing with your own fears of abandonment, guilt and familial duty and loyalty. As well as you might have to deal with internalised core beliefs about that family harmony is more important than your own wellbeing. It is not, but you may still have to deal with those beliefs.

Again, I was utterly terrified when I started to put boundaries in place with my own family because I was scared of being shouted at, hated and being guilt-tripped into submission.

However, there are strategies to help you overcome and deal with resistant family members.

<u>What Are Some Strategies To Deal With Resistant Family Members?</u>

Firstly, you need to start small. This is something my best friend kept banging on about because they could see how distressed and scared I was about setting boundaries, so they encouraged me to start very small. You should start small because this helps make the task of setting boundaries more manageable and then you can gradually build from there. For instance, the only real boundaries I have currently set with my family is something along the lines of *Don't ask me how I am if you aren't going to listen.* That is a very small and manageable boundary that I can and will build on over time.

Think about a small boundary you could set and go from there. Rome wasn't built in a day so neither will boundary setting.

Secondly, you need to be clear and direct. To do this, you should use "I" statements so no one can accuse you of being influenced by other people and you are definitely saying this is what *you* want during this conversation. This is very important in setting your boundaries. For example, you could say the following to your family, "I don't feel comfortable having this conversation right now. I want to take a break and we can talk about this again in the future,"

Thirdly, you need to focus on yourself. As much as I would love to tell you that you can control how others will react that isn't possible and you can only control your own responses as well as actions. It reminds me of something that happened in my friendship group back in May 2024 when a person with persecutory delusions attacked me very publicly and repeatedly over text. I knew right in this moment she was in the wrong for attacking me and I could have ripped into her just as hard but that wouldn't have helped the situation. If I had attacked her back then everything would have gotten a lot worse and there was a very good risk I would become just as guilty as her. My point is what you do when family members are being resistant and possibly attacking you when you go to set boundaries matters. Don't engage, don't make things worse.

If your family members are being resistant and horrible then please, just walk away. You can always return to conversations later on when they are calmer.

Always focus on meeting your own needs and not the needs of others. Sometimes people will change, sometimes they will not so don't waste your energy getting people to change when they will not.

Fourthly, expect pushback. I hope by this point in the podcast episode that you're starting to realise that you will get pushback because toxic family members will not like you setting boundaries and reclaiming your life. Therefore, expect that they're going to manipulate, guilt-trip and use other strategies to try to get you to back down. Yet you need to stay firm, set and enforce those boundaries and take all the time and space you need so you can heal.

This is about you, not them.

Finally, you need to seek support. Not only from a dear friend or non-toxic family member that knows what you're going through, but healing from trauma is hard. It is very possible to heal from trauma but you never have to do it alone. Therefore, please seek support from a therapist, a dear friend and a support group.

Setting boundaries is just one part of the journey towards healing from trauma, but it is a very rewarding part indeed.

<u>Conclusion</u>

Ultimately, when it comes to setting boundaries, it is extremely important to your trauma healing and your life that you never give up. Sure, there will be struggles, setbacks and there will be family members that never want you to set boundaries, but you need to do it for you. You are so much more important than you realise.

Also, it's important to realise, truly realise that healing isn't linear. There will be setbacks, you will dip and you will rise so high that you think the worst is behind you, and that's okay. That is how healing works. I know that better than most.

As a result, I would suggest that you learn from your setbacks and you celebrate your successes. Every single step you take towards healthier boundaries is a step closer towards you creating a space within yourself and within your social world where you can develop self-compassion, post-traumatic growth and you can heal.

Healing is more than possible as much as it seems impossible most of the time, but if you set boundaries then you might be a lot closer to starting to truly heal than you ever thought possible.

WHAT ARE SOCIAL SCRIPTS TO HELP YOU SET FAMILY BOUNDARIES AFTER TRAUMA?

Building upon the last chapter, in this next chapter, you're going to learn the sort of things to say to family members to help set and reinforce your boundaries. I originally wrote the psychology article this chapter is based on a few months ago, and my relationship with my family is so much better now and it is lovely.

That is all because of my boundaries and me reinforcing them, so this can work if you put in the effort, remember your unshakable self and you enforce your boundaries.

What Are Social Scripts Important?

Social scripts are lines or sentences you practise so you know what to say to family members or other people you are trying to set boundaries with. As well as social scripts are sentences you remember so you can counter and practise defending your boundaries against family resistance.

For example, a boundary I want to set is something along the lines of *if you're going to ask me how I am, actually let me talk about how I actually am*. Yet my "social environment" would have a lot of different excuses about why they shouldn't or wouldn't do that. Mostly it boils down to my trauma is too painful for them, so me being depressed, having PTSD and being suicidal at times is too much for them.

Therefore, developing useful and effective social scripts would allow me to come up with a good counterargument or statement.

Ultimately, survivors of developmental trauma typically experience some form of unsafe, unsupportive and unhealthy family dynamics. This is why as a survivor of trauma, you need to establish boundaries with your family to protect yourself and chances are, they will improve your family relationships too. Yet this can feel like one of the hardest things you will ever do.

To be honest, the night my counsellor recommended this to me I had such a bad mental health spiral because I was so terrified of this idea, and I've been uncomfortable about this setting boundaries idea for days now. Thankfully, I see my "social environment" tomorrow so I can set one or two small boundaries then, I seriously hope I can.

As a result in the rest of the podcast episode, we'll going to be looking at some scripts you can use in different situations to help set and reinforce your boundaries.

General Social Scripts

In a moment, we're going to look at some social scripts to protect you and get boundaries during specific topics. Yet I want to start us off with some general social scripts that will help you in everyday conversations if your family members try to disrespect your boundaries.

Some general social scripts are:

- *I don't have to explain myself to you.*
- *I prefer not to say.*
- *No, that's why I'm not going to share.*
- *No.*
- *Silence (just don't say anything)*
- *I can't do this, I'm sorry.*

Scripts For Emotionally Charged Conversations

There are certain conversations that will

be very emotionally charged, causing yourself and/ or your family members to be very emotional and reactive. These conversations can include death, politics, trauma and politics. For example, my "social environment" firmly denies they have ever done anything worse whatsoever, so trauma is a very, very emotionally charged topic. Mainly, it involves a lot of gaslighting.

Although, when it comes to these emotionally charged conversations YOU get to decide how you contribute and interact with these topics. You don't actually have to and then you need to communicate your choices to your family members.

Some possible scripts include:

- *My thoughts and opinions are just as important as yours so if you want me to listen then you need to listen to me as well. Can you do that?*
- *That hasn't been my experience.*
- *Let's agree to disagree*
- *I'm embarrassed that you brought that up in front of everyone. Please talk about this topic in private with me next time.*
- *I'm overwhelmed right now so it's difficult for me to focus on feedback. I need a break.*

Equally, I think a munch of the General Social Scripts are useful here too because if you're talking about trauma or why you don't want to go out and do something. Then you can simply say *I don't have to explain myself to you.* Even though I have to admit because of my trauma that is a really scary idea.

<u>Social Scripts For Safety</u>

For a lot of trauma survivors, safety is a very weird concept because I do feel a lot safer than I used to and I truly understand in my head what safety is, but I don't always feel it. There are only certain situations I feel truly safe in and that no one will hurt me at all, even though I have never actually been physically hurt. There were always the threat because I'm gay but emotional safety is important too. Something I have never really had.

Therefore, you might not feel physically or emotionally safe when you're with your family so you might need to establish boundaries to secure your safety and the safety of other people.

Some Safety Social Scripts can include:

- *I'm not attending that family event if This Person is going.*
- *I'm happy to come but I will not be left alone with This Person.*
- *Whenever I visit you always invalidate me so I feel hurt and unsupported. If you want me to continue visiting hen you need to stop invalidating me.*
- *I'm happy to spend time with you but it has to be outdoors, not indoors.*
- *I know you can take me but I want to drive there myself. That way I can leave when I need to.*
- *No thank you, I don't want to be touched.*

Personally, this is a category I'm going to be focusing on for my own conversations because social stuff is all about safety and I want to feel more comfortable doing social things with my "social environment". Instead of them always invalidating me, my rape and my trauma. As well as I need to get so much better at reinforcing my no-touch-without-permission rule because last time my "social environment" did that, it was bad. And it's an awful example of how my childhood trauma comes up so I'm too scared to reinforce my boundaries.

Social Scripts To Use About Children

Whilst I really want to have children in the future, I don't have any children at the moment. However, a caregiver's main job is to ensure their child is safe and they have good welfare so your family members might or might not be biologically related to your child, they may or may not be closed or expect to be in charge of your child. Yet ultimately, these family members are not responsible for your child.

You are.

As a result, it's up to you to set any boundaries you deem necessary to take care of your child.

Some Social Scripts About Children Include:

- *Do not use those words in front of my child.*
- *That (Specific Thing) is not up for debate when it comes to my child.*
- *As their caregiver, I made the final decision because I am responsible for their welfare and wellbeing.*
- *Thanks for the feedback. I'll deal with it with (other parent or child) and I'll reach out if I need extra feedback.*
- *You can ask my child if they want to hug you but please don't force them. Respect their physical boundaries.*

Conclusion

As a survivor myself of two types of trauma, I understand how scary this is. The idea of setting boundaries with my family that I need to reinforce after 22 years, absolutely terrifies me because it is so new, unknown and I know I am going to be met with so much resistance. Yet I know this is critical to my mental health going forward and I cannot heal from my trauma and my rape without these boundaries being reinforced so it's hard.

Just please give yourself a chance to make these boundaries, enforce them and start to heal. You deserve to have a healthy relationship with your family, regardless of how impossible, scary and intimidating it may seem.

FINDING A SENSE OF WHOLENESS

Ultimately, I think as much as we've spoken about finding our sense of self and trying to become more resilient, so we can build an Unshakable Self. I think the root aspect of our Self that we are trying to find is a sense of wholeness. Since after you've experienced trauma and even more so if you were unloved as a child, there is a terribly big hole left within.

It is what some people call Emotional Dependency and other people call External Locus of Control. It doesn't really matter what you call it, this is one example of how psychological trauma can leave us feeling empty, hallow or like we are missing a critical part of our Self. It took me years to feel whole again after my child abuse and intense homophobic upbringing. Before then I always felt fractured, unloved and like I could never be my full Self. There would always be that sad, terrified, traumatised gay part of my Self.

Thankfully, during my trauma healing, I

managed to reincorporate that terrified part of my Self into my core self and it really did help me to feel whole again.

In addition, I know after my rape, I felt so broken, so shattered and so useless that I grieved. I grieved so much for what he had done to me and everything he had stolen from me.

I'll explain more in an extract from my *What is Rape Grief* article in a moment, but I grieved for my innocence, I grieved for the fear I had that he had taken my virginity, and mostly, I grieved for my Self because I was unable to do so many of the things that I loved doing. As I mentioned before, I couldn't write, I couldn't go out and socialise, I couldn't do anything.

He had stolen all of that from me and he had killed my mental health for so long.

Therefore, when it comes to recovering from trauma and Post-Traumatic Stress Disorder, a lot of survivors, regardless of the type of trauma, grieve for everything that they have lost. Trauma survivors grieve for their lost time, their relationships, their potential, and sometimes we grieve for the loss of peace within ourselves because the shame and guilt is always unbearable.

Personally, some of the other aspects I grieved for, even now to some extent, are the lost friendships. There was a guy who really liked me as a friend and he really pursued our friendship at first, until he learnt that I had been raped. And then I guess he didn't really know how to handle that fact and we still spoke a little, but I could barely do one-on-one stuff and things were different after I revealed that little fact.

He didn't actually ever see my mental health outcomes or my depression or my sheer terrified trauma responses. Even though, when we hugged once, it was way too much and it was the thing that broke my back and caused my mental breakdown. Something that lasted another three months.

Sometimes I wonder what would have happened between us. He was different, cute even and yeah, he was straight but he wanted to be friends. I have other straight friends but I would have liked to still remain friends.

I have another story like that but this other friend did see a few bits and pieces of the impact of my rape on my mental health. And it is tough for some people.

Anyway, I talk more about this in *Breaking The Silence* and *Healing As A Survivor* but it is needed and a critical part of healing to remember, process and "feel" our way through our grief. I always say that you need to deal with your trauma otherwise your trauma will deal with you.

Therefore, grieving is important in trauma healing because it allows us to understand and process what was lost, what we never should have had to go through, what was never realised in our potential and what we have given up because of it. That is all important to our healing.

Peter Walker, LMFT says the following about this "self-sorrowing" type of grief:

"…one of the most beautiful and restorative of emotional experiences. There is nothing in the world more centering than a good unabashed cry about one's troubles. Nothing dissolves the awful abandonment pain of the inner child like a good cry for the self."

What Is Rape Grief?

I think I found the concept of "rape grief"

extremely powerful and important to me because it captured so much of what I was experiencing in the early days after my rape.

Therefore, grief is an intense emotional response to significant personal loss, and this painful emotional experience can include us wanting what we had lost back, concerns and fears about the future, as well as remorse for what we did and didn't do in a given moment. Now everyone experiences grief at some point in their life and it isn't always around death despite popular opinion. For instance, yes, when someone dies we want our loved one back, we get fearful and concerned about how we will deal with them no longer there in the future and we question whether they knew we loved them or not. Equally, when it comes to jobs, we can yearn for that job promotion we never got, we can question if we said the right thing or not in an interview and we might question how we will work at the company now someone else is your boss or got the promotion.

We can experience grief around anything as long as there is that personal loss.

In addition, grief isn't a bad thing. Whilst it is a painful emotional experience, grief is a natural part of our lives and everyone will go through grief at some point in their life. It only becomes a clinical difficulty or "condition" if the grief causes clinically significant levels of psychological distress and impaired functioning in multiple domains of life. Like home life, work and school. As well as if it generates thoughts of self-harm, self-neglect and sometimes grief can be powerful enough to harm our own immune system.

As a result, when it comes to rape and other examples of sexual trauma, this "rape grief" follows the initial shock of the attack. This shock eventually leads to feelings of loss and fear amongst the sexual assault survivors because the survivors can lose a lot because of the attacker. For instance, survivors can feel a loss of their sense of safety and the following too:

- Loss of their lifestyle
- Loss of their physical and mental health.
- Loss of trust in other people
- Loss of their ability to work
- Loss of their hopes and dreams about the future
- Loss of virginity if their rape was their first sexual encounter
- Loss of important relationships. This is mainly if the attacker belongs to their family or group of friends.
- Loss of interest in physical intimacy
- Loss of ability to resume their normal roles like going to school.
- Loss of self-esteem

Personally, I don't believe there was a single one of those bullet points that I haven't experienced myself. Although, I will add in my book, *I Am A Survivor, Not A Victim* I do comment on here I firmly reject the idea that rape counts as losing your virginity. That was a very healing moment for me.

However, during the first 7-months of my rape, I felt a massive sense of loss because I had lost my sense of safety, my sense of hope about the future and the idea that I could ever work again or live a normal life. As well as I completely lost my ability to live my lifestyle and do my normal roles.

Moreover, when we consider how significant and how many of these sense of losses combine, it is no surprise that sexual assault survivors experience rape grief to extreme levels. The process of healing from rape grief isn't linear or easy or straightforward in the slightest. When I consider my own mental health journey, there have been major breakthrough moments where I thought my life was changed and healed forever, then new triggers, new fears and new experiences cause that all to change so this requires more healing. Trauma recovery ebbs and flows and it depends on the triggers that the client experiences as these act as reminders of what the client has lost.

In addition, one of the most annoying things but equally, it was this fact that I found healing. It is the fact that survivors experiencing rape grief will have conflicting emotions. For example, I remember this clearly because I had just found out about rape grief, I was sitting on the ugly red sofas in our shared house and me and my best friend had moved in together whilst the other two didn't until two months later. After a month, we were sitting on the sofa in the afternoon, I was depressed and I wanted to be alone. Yet I wanted to be with my best friend. I wanted to share everything with my best friend including the nightmares about them raping me (my best friend would never ever do that to me) but I didn't want to tell them because it would hurt them. And so many more conflicting emotions and thoughts.

I felt insane half the time.

And it is that simple realisation that it is okay for rape survivors to feel so many conflicting emotions.

It is normal. As difficult, insane and awful as you feel when you're experiencing all these different emotions, you are reacting normally to an extremely abnormal situation

Finding Wholeness After Grief and Trauma

Nonetheless, it is important and if life has taught me anything is that healing is not a slog through endless sadness. As well as whilst all survivors focus on the grief and the sheer sadness that we are experiencing, there is a lot of happiness as well in the odd moments.

It takes a long time to get there but at some point, survivors are able to "self-marvel" after their self-compassion grows. I've already explained the 4 steps of self-compassion so I won't rehash them here, but please do flick back and reread the steps.

In addition, this self-compassion is extra important in healing because when a person has self-compassion. Then they can go through something like a consolidation of their experiences. This is similar to a reunion of the various parts of themselves and their experiences, so they can finally be whole again after their trauma.

Whilst these self-compassion moments can happen at any point (and thankfully they do) of the healing process, this is actually spoken about in the Three-Stage Recovery Model by American psychiatrist Judith Herman in the final stage. Which I'll share a snippet from an article I wrote and link it back to the current topic and your unshakable Self in a moment.

"What is The Reconnection and Integration Stage of The Recovery Model?

In the final stage of the model, therapists work with clients to help them work towards reconnecting with their world as well as integrating their trauma into a new sense of self. For example, during this stage, clients regain trust in their relationships because they've learnt how to extend their trust and when it's best not to extend trust to someone. As well as this stage involves something called "reparenting". I first came across this term in my counselling during August 2023 and this is a term that describes the therapist's role in modelling healthy boundaries as well as relationships. When it comes to trauma survivors, this can include relearning what are, how to have and how to recognise healthy sexual relationships. Something that myself and a lot of different survivors find immensely difficult, because this "reparenting" is often the first time that someone has spoken to us about what on Earth healthy relationships look like.

In addition, a major part of reconnection during this stage is the survivor developing and maintaining their ability to form and sustain healthy relationships. This doesn't only mean sexual relationships, but it can include friendships and familial relationships too. I talk a lot about these aspects of my trauma recovery in my book *Healing As A Survivor.* Also, for survivors of sexual abuse and sexual violence, a lot of survivors have to rediscover their sexual identity and sexual preferences, which is immensely challenging, because this only adds to the struggle that survivors have around their sense of self.

Furthermore, you tend to be able to see progress in this stage of trauma recovery in a few different ways. For instance, as clients progress, they can enjoy intimacy or new experiences without associating it with their abuser or feeling like they need to be protected from their abuser. And the reason why these are amazing, wonderful moments for survivors is because they show the client is growing in their autonomy and ability to live with the fear and trauma responses that have ruled their life for so long.

I know for me, being able to go out with a newish friend one-on-one was an amazing experience, because for the past 7 months that would have been flat out impossible. It would have caused me to have a panic attack, a breakdown and I would have had constant trauma responses. That had happened a good few times.

However, this is a difficult and scary stage of trauma recovery because it's an immensely weird and disorienting feeling to know that you don't need to be protected from your attacker. Also, it is so disorienting to feel safe secure to experience life and pleasure without trauma responses. I talk more about this in my healing book, but I found it weird because I had been having severe PTSD for 7 months and then it wasn't.

It was weird to experience such an extreme change."

Ultimately, after this self-compassion starts to grow and a person consolidates their experiences, pain and Self, these self-marvelling moments begin to find somewhere inside a person, amongst all the self-loathing, all the grief and all the pain, to root down. Then these moments can be great signposts along the healing route to show the person that they are actually making progress.

Personally, until now, I had no idea what to call these moments but they were so important to me during my sexual trauma healing. Of course, there were times when I thought these moments meant I was doing so much better than I actually was, but they were still little hopeful moments in amongst all the darkness, pain and grief.

I remember how happy I was when I was able to go out for lunch one-on-one with a newish friend without my best friend. For seven months, it had been impossible for me to go out and do anything social without my best friend being there. If I did go out without them then my mental health would be wrecked when I got back and I would be in for a hell of a night.

I was so happy when I was able to go out one-on-one with someone else. Of course, I struggled with a lot of other negative mental health outcome afterwards. Yet I knew I was making some progress at the very least.

Speaking of which, when it comes to these self-compassionate moments that overtime allow you to heal and find a sense of wholeness once again. These moments are not single brilliant moments. They are more like moments that make us feel great or at least a little better than we have been for a while. As well as they can be moments that highlight just how much trauma we have endured and just how challenging, painful and much of a struggle our lives have been.

You will likely be painfully aware of just how much negativity and hate and trauma we had to navigate as younger parts of our Self. Even now there are certain queer or relationship or sex topics that pop up when my friends talk about perfectly normal things. Well, it is perfectly normal for them to think or do at that age. Yet if I did, thought or wanted to try or wear a specific thing when I was that young or up until last year, I would have simply been too terrified that I would be killed.

In those moments, I am painfully aware how much I endured as a child.

A child who spent the vast, vast majority of their childhood just surviving and never really knowing what living or being a child meant.

Equally, these self-compassionate moments can be great reminders of how resilient, brilliant and amazing we are. Because we survived.

Despite everything that the world, our culture and our families threw at us, we survived. Also, it is not only us that survived, it is all the parts of our Self from the toddler to the school age or the teenage part of us. They all survived because we are creative, we are determined and we are persevering so that no matter what the world throws at us, we can always survive.

It was likely flat out impossible to survive at times, and it often required ways of learning and ways of escape. Like through school, art, music, books and whatever other ways we could figure out.

However, none of that matters because we managed to survive all our trauma somehow, and we managed to ensure all the parts of our Self survived too. Sure, our Self might be a little fractured, a little disjointed and some parts of the Self might have been harmed more than others. They are still alive though.

As a result, when it comes to self-marvelling, just like in Internal Family Therapy, we can connect with the exiled younger parts of our Self and we can reclaim them. We can reparent and help our sense of Self become whole again where there are no more exiled parts and we can be united again as one singular Self.

Peter Walker, Richard Schwartz and Internal Family Therapy and likely many more focus on this sort of therapeutic work for trauma survivors, so if this sounds like something you resonate with then please explore it further.

At the end of this chapter, I just wanted to stress that feeling whole is amazing and I do believe it is a core part of having a strong Self. If you have united all the parts of our Self after trauma then it is only then that you'll be able to become more resilient, who you are and process more about your values.

So much of this book cannot be done if you are not whole, if you have not processed your trauma and if you have not grieved for everything you have lost.

My questions at the end of this chapter are:

- Do you feel a sense of wholeness?
- If you've experienced trauma, what do you grieve about?
- If you don't feel a sense of wholeness, can you name the parts of your Self that feel disconnected?
- How can you reunite your Self?

CONCLUSION

"As long as I have my unshakable self, I can dig in with both feet with all my might. As long as I know who I am, all my doubts, hesitations, and frustrations will disappear. And no demon on earth can escape my descending blade,"

Just as I started this book, I wanted to end with this brilliant quote because we have looked at a lot of great topics in this book. We have learnt about the importance of knowing who you are, the mental health benefits of knowing yourself and so much more.

In addition, I wanted to start this conclusion with a brief caveat. Even though this entire book is focused on building your Unshakable Self, please note that you will still have tough days. This book is not a magic bullet that means you will never have a bad day ever again.

The knowledge, questions and all the personal experiences I've included in this book are a guide to help you overtime. It takes time, a lot of healing and a lot of self-acceptance to build your Unshakable Self.

You will still have bad days, you will still get upset and you might still struggle with challenges that life throws at you. Yet by knowing who you are, you'll be better able to adapt, change and deal with whatever life has to throw at you.

Personally, knowing who I am after healing from both forms of trauma has been extremely powerful and helpful. If my counsellor and myself didn't work on building my Self so I knew I was so much more than my trauma and my anorexia then I would have just continued the cycle I've been doing for the past twenty-three years. I would have continued a cycle of bad mental health, experiencing anorexia and so much more.

Until maybe one day I wouldn't be here.

However, because I know who I am, I know I am a strong person with the core values of creativity, independence, life-long learning, supportive and curiosity. I can make decisions that make me happy and support my mental health going forward.

I've already made a lot of positive changes

to my life based on knowing who I am, besides my anorexia, and I am reaping the rewards. The benefits of having my Unshakable Self have made my friendships, relationships, work and so many other aspects of my life better too.

Therefore, at the end of this book, I just want to finish by saying, I've included a lot of questions at the end of the chapters and you've learnt a lot of knowledge. If you haven't done the questions yet then I highly recommend that you do them because they will be really helpful to you.

And finally, go out into the world, find your Unshakable Self and know who you are. You'll probably find it even more rewarding, brilliant and fun than you ever thought possible.

I know I did.

So my final question for you is, *who are you?*

REFERENCES AND FURTHER READING

Adams, G. R., & Marshall, S. K. (1996). A developmental social psychology of identity: Understanding the person-in-context. Journal of adolescence, 19(5), 429-442.

Agroskin, D., Klackl, J., & Jonas, E. (2014). The self-liking brain: a VBM study on the structural substrate of self-esteem. PloS one, 9(1), e86430.

Baltes, M. M., & Silverberg, S. B. (2019). The dynamics between dependency and autonomy: Illustrations across the life span. In *Life-span development and behavior* (pp. 41-90). Routledge.

Bamberg, M. (2011). Who am I? Narration and its contribution to self and identity. *Theory & psychology*, *21*(1), 3-24.

Bandura, A. (1977). Self-efficacy: Toward a unifying theory of behavioral change. Psychological Review, 84(2), 191-215.

Bırni, G., & Eryılmaz, A. (2024). Conceptual and theoretical review of self-worth. *Psikiyatride Güncel Yaklaşımlar*, *16*(2), 327-346.

Blascovich, J., & Tomaka, J. (1991). Measures of self-esteem. Measures of Personality and Social Psychological Attitudes, 1, 115-160.

Bogee, Jr., L. (1998). Leadership through personal awareness. University of Hawaii. Retrieved from http://www.hawaii.edu/intlrel/LTPA/selfwort.htm

Boyraz, G., Waits. J.B. and Felix, V.A. (2014), 'Authenticity, life satisfaction and distress: A longitudinal analysis', Journal of Counseling Psychology, 61, 498–505.

Brewer, B. (1995). Bodily awareness and the self. *The body and the self*, 291-309.

Brown, K. W., & Ryan, R. M. (2003). The benefits of being present: Mindfulness and its role in psychological well-being. Journal of Personality and Social Psychology, 84(4), 822-848.

Chang, J. J., Ji, Y., Li, Y. H., Yuan, M. Y., & Su, P. Y. (2021). Childhood trauma and depression in college students: Mediating and moderating effects of psychological resilience. *Asian Journal of Psychiatry*, *65*, 102824.

Chen, S., Boucher, H., & Kraus, M. W. (2011). The relational self. *Handbook of identity theory and research*, 149-175.

Choi, K. J., & Kangas, M. (2020). Impact of maternal betrayal trauma on parent and child well-being: Attachment style and emotion regulation as moderators. Psychological

Trauma: Theory, Research, Practice, and Policy, 12(2), 121.

Chryssochoou, X. (2003). Studying identity in social psychology: Some thoughts on the definition of identity and its relation to action. Journal of language and Politics, 2(2), 225-241.

Clark-Jones, T. (2012). The importance of helping teens discover self-worth. Michigan State University – MSU Extension.

Coleman, J. (2024). Rules of Estrangement: Why Adult Children Cut Ties & How to Heal the Conflict. Random House.

Cottle, T. J. (2002). On narratives and the sense of self. *Qualitative Inquiry*, *8*(5), 535-549.

Covington, M. V., & Beery, R. G. (1976). Self-worth and school learning. Oxford, UK: Holt, Rinehart & Winston.

Crawford, E., Liebling-Kalifani, H., & Hill, V. (2009). Women's understanding of the effects of domestic abuse: The impact on their identity, sense of self and resilience. A grounded theory approach. Journal of international women's studies, 11(2), 63-82.

Crocker, J., & Wolfe, C. T. (2001). Contingencies of self-worth. Psychological Review, 108(3), 593.

Crocker, J., Luhtanen, R. K., Cooper, M. L., & Bouvrette, A. (2003). Contingencies of self-worth in college students: Theory and measurement. Journal of Personality and Social Psychology, 85, 894–908.

Darvishnia, A., Aghayousefi, A., & Gharamaleki, N. S. (2023). The effectiveness of coping therapy on domestic violence and selfefficacy in abused women. Journal of Fundamentals of Mental Health, 25(4).

De Luna, J. E., & Wang, D. C. (2021). Child traumatic stress and the sacred: Neurobiologically informed interventions for therapists and parents. Religions, 12(3), 163.

Deaton, J. D., Wymer, B., & Carlson, R. G. (2021). Supervision strategies to facilitate vicarious post traumatic growth among trauma counselors. Journal of Counselor Preparation and Supervision, 14(4), 12.

Deutsch, R., Drozd, L., & Ajoku, C. (2020). Trauma-informed interventions in parent–child contact cases. Family Court Review, 58(2), 470-487.

Dhawan, M., & Kour, P. (2024). Role Of Emotional Intelligence And Self-Esteem On Social Anxiety Among College Students. Educational Administration: Theory and Practice, 30(4), 8609-8616.

Dong, C., Xu, R., & Xu, L. (2021). Relationship of childhood trauma, psychological resilience, and family resilience among undergraduate nursing students: A cross-sectional study. *Perspectives in Psychiatric Care*, *57*(2), 852-859.

Durwood, L., McLaughlin, K. A., & Olson, K. R. (2017). Mental health and self-worth in socially transitioned transgender youth. *Journal of the American Academy of Child & Adolescent Psychiatry*, *56*(2), 116-123.

Erikson, E. H. (1968). Identity: Youth and Crisis. Norton & Co.

Estévez, A., Chávez-Vera, M. D., Momeñe, J., Olave, L., Vázquez, D., & Iruarrizaga, I. (2018). The role of emotional dependence in the relationship between attachment and impulsive behavior.

Evans, J. A., Krumrei-Mancuso, E. J., & Rouse, S. V. (2024). What you are hiding could be hurting you: Autistic masking in relation to mental health, interpersonal trauma, authenticity, and self-esteem. Autism in Adulthood, 6(2), 229-240.

Faelens, L., Hoorelbeke, K., Cambier, R., Van Put, J., Van de Putte, E., De Raedt, R., & Koster, E. H. (2021). The relationship between Instagram use and indicators of mental health: A systematic review. Computers in Human Behavior Reports, 4, 100121.

Feltham C and Dryden W (1993) *Dictionary of Counselling*, Whurr Publishers

Festinger, L. (1954). A theory of social comparison processes. Human Relations, 7(2), 117-140.

Firestone, L. (2014). Essential tips for building true self-worth. Psych Alive.

Fishbane, M. D. (2001). Relational narratives of the self. *Family process*, *40*(3), 273-291.

Flynn, D. M., & Chow, P. (2017). Self-efficacy, self-worth and stress. *Education*, *138*(1), 83-88.

Freud, S. (1923). The Ego and the Id. The Hogarth Press Ltd.

Gallese, V., & Sinigaglia, C. (2010). The bodily self as power for action. *Neuropsychologia*, *48*(3), 746-755.

Gao, X., Zhong, J., Li, H., Pei, Y., Li, X., Zhang, S., ... & Xiong, X. (2023). The relationship between perfectionism, self-perception of orofacial appearance, and mental health in college students. Frontiers in Public Health, 11, 1154413.

Gonzales, A. L., & Hancock, J. T. (2011). Mirror, mirror on my Facebook wall: Effects of exposure to Facebook on self-esteem. Cyberpsychology, Behavior, and Social Networking, 14(1-2), 79-83.

Grande, D. (2018). Building self-esteem and improving relationships. Psychology Today.

Guenther, C. L., Zhang, Y., & Sedikides, C. (2024). The authentic self is the self-enhancing self: A self-enhancement framework of authenticity. Personality and social psychology bulletin, 50(8), 1182-1196.

Haddock, S. A., Weiler, L. M., Trump, L. J., & Henry, K. L. (2017). The efficacy of internal family systems therapy in the treatment of depression among female college students: A pilot study. *Journal of marital and family therapy*, *43*(1), 131-144.

Harris, M., Allardyce, S., & Findlater, D. (2021). Child sexual abuse and Covid-19: Side effects of changed societies and positive lessons for prevention. Criminal Behaviour and Mental Health, 31(5), 289.

Harter, S. (1999). The Construction of the Self: A Developmental Perspective. Guilford Press.

Haslam, C., Haslam, S. A., Jetten, J., Cruwys, T., & Steffens, N. K. (2021). Life change, social identity, and health. Annual Review of Psychology, 72(1), 635-661.

Hibbert, C. (2013). Self-esteem vs. self-worth. Dr. Christina Hibbert.

Hilbert, S., Goerigk, S., Padberg, F., Nadjiri, A., Übleis, A., Jobst, A., Dewald-Kaufmann, J., Falkai, P., Bühner, M., Naumann, F., & Sarubin, N. (2019). The Role of Self-Esteem in Depression: A Longitudinal Study. Behavioural and cognitive psychotherapy, 47(2), 244–250.

Howard, J. A. (2000). Social psychology of identities. Annual review of sociology, 26(1), 367-393.

https://www.healthyplace.com/blogs/buildingselfesteem/2012/05/the-difference-between-self-esteem-and-self-confidence

https://www.livewellwithsharonmartin.com/boundaries-healing-childhood-trauma

https://www.psychologytoday.com/us/blog/anger-in-the-age-entitlement/201406/how-much-do-you-value-yourself

https://www.psychologytoday.com/us/blog/evolution-the-self/201904/are-you-too-emotionally-dependent-your-partner

James, W. (1890). The Principles of Psychology. Henry Holt and Company.

Jantz, G. L. P. D., & McMurray, A. (2013). Hope and healing from emotional abuse. Baker Books.

Joseph, S. (2016). Authentic. How to be yourself and why it matters. Piatkus. London.

Kaplan, A. (1986). The" self-in-relation": Implications for depression in women. Psychotherapy: Theory, Research, Practice, Training, 23(2), 234.

Karakitsiou, G., Plakias, S., Kedraka, K., Arvaniti, A., Kokkotis, C., Tsiakiri, A., & Samakouri, M. (2023). Investigating the role of second chance schools and COVID-19 pandemic on the mental health and self-image of Greek adult students. Brain sciences, 13(8), 1203.

Kopala-Sibley, D. C., & Zuroff, D. C. (2020). The self and depression: Four psychological theories and their potential neural correlates. Journal of personality, 88(1), 14–30. https://doi.org/10.1111/jopy.12456

Koskina, N., & Giovazolias, T. (2018). The effect of attachment insecurity in the development of eating disturbances across gender: The role of body dissatisfaction. In *Marital Relationships and Parenting: Intimate relations and their correlates* (pp. 191-213). Routledge.

Kouvelis, G., & Kangas, M. (2021). Evaluating the association between interpersonal trauma and self-identity: A systematic review. Traumatology, 27(2), 118.

Kriakous, S. A., Elliott, K. A., Lamers, C., & Owen, R. (2021). The effectiveness of mindfulness-based stress reduction on the psychological functioning of healthcare professionals: A systematic review. Mindfulness, 12, 1-28.

Lamont, M. (2019). From 'having'to 'being': Self-worth and the current crisis of American society. *The British journal of sociology*, *70*(3), 660-707.

Liao, J., Xia, T., Xu, X., & Pan, L. (2023). The effect of appearance anxiety on social anxiety among college students: sequential mediating effects of self-efficacy and self-esteem. Behavioral Sciences, 13(8), 692.

Lopez, R. B., & Polletta, I. (2021). Regulating self-image on Instagram: Links between social anxiety, Instagram contingent self-worth, and content control behaviors. Frontiers in Psychology, 12, 711447.

Lucero, R., Jones, A. C., & Hunsaker, J. C. (2018). Using internal family systems theory in the treatment of combat veterans with post-traumatic stress disorder and their families. *Contemporary Family Therapy*, *40*, 266-275.

Markus, H. R., & Kitayama, S. (1991). Culture and the self: Implications for cognition, emotion, and motivation. Psychological Review, 98(2), 224-253.

Martin, M. G. F. (1995). Bodily awareness: A sense of ownership. *The body and the self*, 267-

289.

Mason, T. B., Smith, K. E., Engwall, A., Lass, A., Mead, M., Sorby, M., Bjorlie, K., Strauman, T. J., & Wonderlich, S. (2019). Self-discrepancy theory as a transdiagnostic framework: A meta-analysis of self-discrepancy and psychopathology. Psychological bulletin, 145(4), 372–389.

Merino, M., Tornero-Aguilera, J. F., Rubio-Zarapuz, A., Villanueva-Tobaldo, C. V., Martín-Rodríguez, A., & Clemente-Suárez, V. J. (2024, July). Body perceptions and psychological well-being: A review of the impact of social media and physical measurements on self-esteem and mental health with a focus on body image satisfaction and its relationship with cultural and gender factors. In Healthcare (Vol. 12, No. 14, p. 1396). MDPI.

Mojta, C., Falconier, M. K., & Huebner, A. J. (2014). Fostering self-awareness in novice therapists using internal family systems therapy. *The American Journal of Family Therapy*, *42*(1), 67-78.

Moretti, M. M., & Higgins, E. T. (1990). Relating self-discrepancy to self-esteem: The contribution of discrepancy beyond acutal-self ratings. Journal of Experimental Social Psychology, 26(2), 108–123.

Nartova-Bochaver, S., Reznichenko, S., & Maltby, J. (2021). The authenticity scale: validation in Russian culture. Frontiers in psychology, 11, 609617.

Nurick, J. (2024). Heal Your Anxious Attachment: Release Past Trauma, Cultivate Secure Relationships, and Nurture a Deeper Sense of Self. New Harbinger Publications.

Ochs, E., & Capps, L. (1996). Narrating the self. *Annual review of anthropology*, *25*(1), 19-43.

Raghavan, S., & Sandanapitchai, P. (2020). The relationship between cultural variables and resilience to psychological trauma: A systematic review of the literature. *Traumatology*.

Ranga, A. (2023). Self-Worth as a Predictor of Mental Health Among Emerging Adults.

Rauch, S. A. M., & Rothbaum, B. O. (2023). *Making Meaning of Difficult Experiences: A Self-Guided Program*. Oxford University Press. https://doi.org/10.1093/med-psych/9780197642573.001.0001

Roeckner, A. R., Oliver, K. I., Lebois, L. A. M., van Rooij, S. J. H., & Stevens, J. S. (2021). Neural contributors to trauma resilience: a review of longitudinal neuroimaging studies. *Translational Psychiatry*, *11*(1), 508. https://doi.org/10.1038/s41398-021-01633-y

Rogers C (1951) *Client-Centered Therapy*, Constable

Rogers, C. R. (1959). A Theory of Therapy, Personality, and Interpersonal Relationships: As Developed in the Client-Centered Framework. In S. Koch (Ed.), Psychology: A Study of a Science. Vol. 3: Formulations of the Person and the Social Context. McGraw-Hill.

Rothbaum, B. O., & Rauch, S. A. M. (2020). *PTSD: What everyone needs to know*. Oxford University Press.

Saha, S., Chung, M. C., & Thorne, L. (2011). A narrative exploration of the sense of self of women recovering from childhood sexual abuse. Counselling Psychology Quarterly, 24(2), 101-113.

Schwartz, R. C. (2013). Moving from acceptance toward transformation with internal family systems therapy (IFS). *Journal of clinical psychology*, *69*(8), 805-816.

Schwartz, R. C., & Sweezy, M. (2019). *Internal family systems therapy*. Guilford Publications.

Shadick, N. A., Sowell, N. F., Frits, M. L., Hoffman, S. M., Hartz, S. A., Booth, F. D., ... & Schwartz, R. C. (2013). A randomized controlled trial of an internal family systems-based psychotherapeutic intervention on outcomes in rheumatoid arthritis: a proof-of-concept study. *The Journal of rheumatology*, *40*(11), 1831-1841.

Sicinski, A. (n.d.). How to build self-worth and start believing in yourself again. IQ Matrix.

Song, S., Yang, X., Yang, H., Zhou, P., Ma, H., Teng, C., ... & Zhang, N. (2021). Psychological resilience as a protective factor for depression and anxiety among the public during the outbreak of COVID-19. *Frontiers in psychology*, *11*, 618509.

Spears, R. (2021). Social influence and group identity. Annual review of psychology, 72(1), 367-390.

Strauman, T. J., & Higgins, E. T. (1987). Automatic activation of self-discrepancies and emotional syndromes: when cognitive structures influence affect. Journal of personality and social psychology, 53(6), 1004–1014.

Strauman, T. J., & Higgins, E. T. (1988). Self-discrepancies as predictors of vulnerability to distinct syndromes of chronic emotional distress. Journal of personality, 56(4), 685–707

Suh, E. M. (2007). Downsides of an overly context-sensitive self: Implications from the culture and subjective well-being research. *Journal of personality*, *75*(6), 1321-1343.

Tolan J (2003) *Skills in Person-Centred Counselling & Psychotherapy*, Sage

Troy, A. S., Willroth, E. C., Shallcross, A. J., Giuliani, N. R., Gross, J. J., & Mauss, I. B. (2023). Psychological resilience: an affect-regulation framework. *Annual review of psychology*, *74*(1), 547-576.

Türk-Kurtça, T., & Kocatürk, M. (2020). The Role of Childhood Traumas, Emotional Self-Efficacy and Internal-External Locus of Control in Predicting Psychological Resilience. *International Journal of Education and Literacy Studies*, *8*(3), 105-115.

Vannini, P., Waskul, D., & Gottschalk, S. (2013). *The senses in self, society, and culture: A sociology of the senses*. Routledge.

Wang, Y. N. (2016). Balanced authenticity predicts optimal well-being: Theoretical conceptualization and empirical development of the authenticity in relationships scale. Personality and Individual Differences, 94, 316-323. doi:10.1016/j.paid.2016.02.001

Wark, L., Thomas, M., & Peterson, S. (2001). Internal family systems therapy for children in family therapy. *Journal of marital and family therapy*, *27*(2), 189-200.

Whitbourne, S.K. (2010). The search for fulfillment. New York: Ballantine Books

Wong, S. J. (n.d.). 13 things that don't determine your self-worth. Shine.

Wood, K. M. (2023). Setting Boundaries: 100 Ways to Protect Yourself, Strengthen Your Relationships, and Build the Life You Want... Starting Now!. Simon and Schuster.

Sign Up Bonus

Keep up to date with exclusive deals on Connor Whiteley's Books, as well as the latest news about new releases and so much more!

Sign up to get a FREE psychology book boxset.

Sign Up Now!

https://www.subscribepage.com/psychologyboxset

Subscriptions:

Never miss an issue!

3 Month Subscription… $19.99

6 Month Subscription… $39.99

12 Month Subscription… $69.99

Subscribe Up Now!

https://payhip.com/b/eoQ85

www.ingramcontent.com/pod-product-compliance
Lightning Source LLC
LaVergne TN
LVHW082344200926
848481LV00012B/3452
* 9 7 8 1 9 1 8 5 9 9 7 4 9 *